CHEFS ON THE FARM

CHEFS
ON THE FARM

Recipes and Inspiration
from the Quillisascut Farm School
of the Domestic Arts

Shannon Borg AND Lora Lea Misterly

RECIPES BY Kären Jurgensen
PHOTOGRAPHY BY Harley Soltes

FOREWORD BY Tom Douglas

SKIPSTONE

© 2008 by Shannon Borg and Lora Lea Misterly
Recipes © 2008 by Kären Jurgensen
Foreword © 2008 by Tom Douglas
Photography © 2008 by Harley Soltes

Published by Skipstone, an imprint of The Mountaineers Books
Printed in China

First printing 2008
11 10 09 08   5 4 3 2 1

Copy Editor: Amy Smith Bell
Design: Karen Schober
Cover photograph: *Farmer Rick Misterly gathers Oregon Spring tomatoes, some of the many heirloom and open-pollinated varieties grown on Quillisascut Farm.*
Pages 2-3 photograph: *Snow blankets a field of wheat stubble on a plateau above the Columbia River.*
Pages 6-7 photograph: *Rick rolls out a bale of alfalfa hay as part of his morning goat feeding ritual.*

ISBN 13: 978-1-59485-080-6

Library of Congress Cataloging-in-Publication Data

Borg, Shannon.
Chefs on the farm : recipes and inspiration from the Quillisascut Farm School of the Domestic Arts / by Shannon Borg and Lora Lea Misterly; recipes by Kären Jurgensen; photography by Harley Soltes; foreword by Tom Douglas.
      p. cm.
Includes index.
ISBN-13: 978-1-59485-080-6 (pbk.)
ISBN-10: 1-59485-080-1 (pbk.)
1. Cookery (Natural foods) 2. Organic farming. 3. Sustainable agriculture.
4. Quillisascut Farm School of the Domestic Arts. I.
Misterly, Lora Lea. II. Jurgensen, Kären, chef. III. Quillisascut Farm School of the Domestic Arts. IV. Title.
TX741.B625 2008
641.5'636—dc22

                    2008009659

Skipstone books may be purchased for corporate, educational, or other promotional sales. For special discounts and information, contact our Sales Department at 1-800-553-4453 or mbooks@mountaineersbooks.org.

Skipstone
1001 SW Klickitat Way
Suite 201
Seattle, Washington 98134
206-223-6303
www.skipstonepress.org
www.mountaineersbooks.org

LIVE LIFE. MAKE RIPPLES.

To our grandmothers and mothers,
Wilma, Sarah, Daisy Mae, and Louise—and all who nurture the cycle of life,
food culture, and the creative spirit

CONTENTS

FOREWORD

IN 1982 I WAS MERRILY RUNNING THE CAFÉ SPORT restaurant in Seattle when an unusual-looking young man knocked at the back door. He had long, greasy hair and a gimpy left leg. He wore a ragged and damp wool sweater and worn-out Birkenstocks, and he smelled of patchouli. In his arms he held a box filled with bags of wild greens and flowers the likes of which I had never eaten or even seen or heard of before. This forager went on to eloquently and methodically explain what each and every green was, where it came from, and what its flavor profile was. He then offered to sell me his wares for a dollar per portion. Sounds cheap today, but at the time we were spending less than twenty-five cents per portion for salad greens. I took the plunge and bought the whole kit and caboodle. Onto the menu these greens went, to be served with a disk of warm, pecan-coated chèvre and a splash of olive oil and lemon. I sold every one of my "Wild Green Salads" that evening and never looked back. From that day on, my priorities were crystallized: I embraced a newfound resolve to change how chefs do business.

Rick and Lora Lea Misterly have played an important part in this transformation among both restaurants and home chefs from "What's available from the corporate produce house?" to the big three buzz words of "What's local, sustainable, and organic?" For many of the young chefs working in my joints, there's a keen curiosity about the farm-to-table connection and a great desire to learn about food that comes from the land—*not* the supermarket shelf. Since 1987, the Misterlys have embraced this concept like few others in Washington State. Each year our business has dedicated itself, and its dollars, to these beliefs—through scholarships that allow interested staff to attend Rick and Lora Lea's Quillisascut Farm School. There, students learn to milk goats, gather eggs, butcher animals, make cheese, and, of course, eat delicious meals cooked from the fruits of their own labors. This has been a life-changing experience for those lucky enough to attend the farm school.

Maybe there's a bit of the farmer in all of us. I never thought I'd see the day when I would be stooped over in the 95-degree summer heat, picking green beans from bushy shrubs and driving cases of produce back to my Seattle restaurants. But since my wife, Jackie, and I recently bought a small farm in the beautiful Yakima Valley, here I am for at least part of every summer. Courageous, hard-working souls like Rick and Lora Lea who make farming their life's work—24/7, year-round—are my heroes. The existence of the Quillisascut Farm School makes life in the Pacific Northwest a little richer, a little greener, and a little more passionate for all of us.

—TOM DOUGLAS

A harvester samples table grapes.

LIST OF RECIPES

BREAKFAST & BREADS

SOUPS & SALADS

ENTRÉES

SIDE DISHES

DESSERTS

PANTRY ITEMS

INTRODUCTION:
ONE LITTLE FARM

WE HOPE THIS BOOK serves as a field guide to what is happening in the small-farm and local sustainable agriculture movement across the United States and throughout the world. More poetry than politics, it offers the tale of Quillisascut Farm, in eastern Washington, as an allegory—one farm that could represent Anyfarm USA—for what can happen and *is* happening across the country in resistance to industrialized agriculture and to the fast-food trend that is consuming our culture. Here at the farm, and at countless other small farms, great things are happening: people are connecting, planting and growing native foods, teaching each other and the next generation, saving seeds, caring humanely for animals, talking to their neighbors and friends about heirloom varieties and their grandmothers' and grandfathers' recipes, and enjoying the conviviality that comes from cooking and eating together.

In growing numbers, farmers, ranchers, and fisherpeople are transporting their harvests to more than forty-four hundred farmers markets (and counting) across the United States. Urban apartment dwellers are riding their bikes or walking to these contemporary agoras to exchange wealth for beauty, flavor, and pleasure. Diners in restaurants are asking, Who grew these potatoes? Who caught this fish? Who made this cheese? Chefs and servers are answering with the names of their friends and colleagues, those dedicated souls who are passionate about food, wine, beer, cheese, beef, fish, oysters, fruits, nuts, and vegetables. They are willing to take the risks necessary to obtain the best possible products. Children are visiting farms and growing tomatoes in their school gardens. "Eaters"—we like to call them "eaters" or "coproducers," as the eco-gastronomic organization Slow Food calls us, rather than "consumers," because we are *all* contributing to our food system—are shopping at specialty stores and large "natural" markets, the subject of growing controversy. People are willing to pay more for the products of the delicate, complex, yet eye-openingly simple food system that gives back so much more than a drive-through burger or a microwaved meal.

In cities across the country, people are eager to know more about the system that delivers their food. They want to become involved in this process, but not many of us have had the chance. As the "fermentation experimentalist" Sandor Ellix Katz wrote in his recent book *The Revolution Will Not Be Microwaved: Inside America's Underground Food Movements:* "I feel lucky to have grown up in a household with a garden, to have watched meals form around ripe vegetables and not just shopping lists generated from abstract desires. I met so many people—people who love food and cooking—who are utterly clueless about what grows when and are completely disempowered in the green world of the garden."

We hope that this book—organized by season and by the yearly cycle of the farm—can empower those who are eager to be a part of the unmicrowavable revolution. It's a handbook for the farmer, the foodie, and the fool alike. It's a record of one very small, if optimistic, part of the local and sustainable agriculture movement. The Quillisascut Farm School of the Domestic Arts, established and run by the farm's owners, Lora Lea and Rick Misterly, is truly a community of farmers, chefs, food lovers, and eaters—from Rice, Colville, and Spokane in eastern Washington to Seattle, San Francisco,

New York, France, and Italy. It grew from a simple idea, like a pebble dropped into nearby Lake Roosevelt rippling outward: that a farm is more than merely a place where our meals are "produced"; that a farm is a home, a place of teaching, a gathering place; and that experiencing a farm's life can change our own.

Quillisascut Farm—appropriately named from a Salish word meaning "place of scattered bushes," since this area of bare, rolling hills and upland steppe is dry in summer and freezing in winter—has been transformed by Rick and Lora Lea into a fertile farm as well as a growing community of people who share a common fascination with the life and lessons of the source of their food. That, and getting up at five AM to milk the goats. Those who come here, from celebrity chefs at top urban restaurants to first-year culinary students, get their hands dirty—literally and willingly—to experience "the force that through the green fuse drives the flower," as the poet Dylan Thomas wrote, the natural energy and passion behind the food and the life they have chosen.

Is it enough? Not at all. Much more local, regional, national, and global work and education need to be done on many cultural, political, and economic levels to combat the processed, fast-food world that has become the norm in the United States and, alarmingly and increasingly, around the world. The road toward a completely sustainable food system in this or any other country is surely a long one. This book is an attempt to share the experiences from only one little farm and to show what one community is learning along the way. Please join us on this culinary and cultural adventure. We hope to see you at the farmers market discussing mushrooms, across an herb-bedecked balcony picking rosemary, or even at five AM in the milking shed at Quillisascut. The goats will be happy to see you, too.

WINTER
DREAMING

FROM THANKSGIVING THROUGH LATE APRIL, almost six months, Quillisascut Farm is dormant on the surface; but below ground it's working, conserving energy, and getting ready for the next season. Winter is a beginning. In the middle of a cold, dry eastern Washington winter, especially on a small farm like this one, time seems to slow down. It's as if everything—the plants, the goats, the chickens, even the soil—is waiting to see what comes next. And the human members of this scene are waiting, too, for the slow season to pass.

"When the first killing frost comes in fall, you feel like you've lost your friends," says farmer and goat-cheese maker Lora Lea Misterly over a cup of tea in the bunkhouse kitchen on a snowy January afternoon. "The abundance is gone—the beans, the tomatoes. We've butchered the lambs. But then you start planning, thinking, and dreaming about next summer. Winter is an incredibly important time for us." By "us," Lora Lea means herself and her husband, fellow farmer Rick, but she's also thinking of the other residents of the farm—about forty Alpine Cross goats that do the majority of the "work" around this place, as well as a smattering of chickens, ducks, cats, and the farm's dogs—Libby, the white-dreadlocked komondor, and Jet, an eager border collie. She also would include every vegetable, tuber,

fruit tree, grapevine, and worm on this land. "Everything is connected here," Lora Lea says. "The soil feeds the plants that feed us. We are merely the walking, talking result of that connection."

This is a different season in which to feel that connection. Most people visit Quillisascut and other farms in summer, when the fields are ripe, the animals graze, and the farm yards buzz with activity. The Quillisascut Farm School of the Domestic Arts is in session then, too, when the garden is full to bursting with enough vegetables, fruits, and herby things to keep dozens of inventive chefs occupied and fed for weeks. Chef Kären Jurgensen is in the kitchen at the farm school every day; she keeps the students busy creating menus and meals, preserving fruit, and breaking down newly butchered animals. Lora Lea invites a steady stream of local farmers, ranchers, and other providers to visit and, in turn, takes the students to visit neighboring farms to help them understand the diversity and interconnectedness of her community. And, of course, Quillisascut is just like farms and farming communities across the country, living through seasonal cycles and making ends meet while producing the food we all eat.

To see the farm in winter is a stark contrast to its summer abundance. Outside, there are two feet of snow; everything is covered and huge, fluffy flakes are adding to the blanket. Inside, the large, bright kitchen is warm. A unique wood-stove-and-pipe system sends hot water through pipes Rick embedded in the concrete floors, keeping the place toasty. Even so, the house seems to be holding its breath, waiting. But Lora Lea knows that although winter on the farm seems quiet, a lot is going on; it's just more subtle than the crazy excesses of summer.

The farm is silent in the insulating snow. Somehow this silence simplifies everything here. The large straw-bale bunkhouse with its salmon-colored stucco and red metal roof—

Hoppy, ready to protect the herd from predators, shows off his rack of horns.

built by Rick, Lora Lea, and friends as a place for the chefs and students to stay when they visit—is a bright contrast to the snow. Behind it on a large patio, the white-stucco-and-brick wood-burning oven looks like an altar. It truly is one—a transformative place where countless pizzas and loaves of bread have been baked. (Miraculous rumors of as many as 120 loaves baked here in a single day circulate even in the restaurant kitchens of Seattle, three hundred miles away.)

Up a small hill stands the weathered brown barn where the goats, chickens, and other animals are hunkered down to ride out this most recent January storm. Nearby, the cheesemaking shed—two rooms devoted to milk storage, and making and aging cheese, big enough for a dozen students to work in—now stands empty. Gardens surround these outbuildings, as well as a small vineyard and orchard, neither of which has been pruned yet, and the gnarled vines look like old trolls, their long canes draping to the ground like hair. Rick and Lora Lea's house, and another small house closer to the road, where Daisy Mae Boughey, Lora Lea's mother, lives, seem almost hidden. In all, most of the square footage of the buildings is devoted to the work of the farm. The farm itself is where the living goes on, year-round.

In the field below, a flock of two dozen Western Merriam wild turkeys bob toward the wooded hills—forward and back, almost single file, like a conga line in their black-and-white-feathered best. The chickens and goats are huddled inside the barn, but they chuckle and stir as they hear Lora Lea approach and open the gate. They're hoping for some tidbit, but also they seem curious, as though they don't want to miss anything.

The garden is a study in white and grey. Snow covers the mounded rows where a few months ago chard and kale, tomatoes and beans prospered in bright abundance. Now ocher-colored corn stalks speckled with black mold are bent over in their rows like piles of bones. Spiky sunflower stalks echo the grey-brown of the wooden fences. From the roof of the cheese shed, four-foot icicles reach halfway to the ground; it has been freezing cold on and off for weeks.

You can see things in winter that would go unnoticed during other times of the year. Here and there in the snow, small piles of jet-black, perfectly egg-shaped rabbit scat mark the paths of those quiet creatures, now snug in their burrows, sleeping the day away. Delicate deer tracks cross the property. Several old rusted farm implements stand out against the white like sculptures from another age. Round, black walnut pods stain the snow beneath their mother tree. A single, fluffy grey turkey feather stands out against a drift, its flat tip darker than the downy pinfeathers closer to the quill end.

Beyond the farm, the foothills of the Huckleberry Mountain range are soft, rolling, scattered with ponderosa pine, tamarack, Western larch, red fir, and the red branches of willow. The scene here is repeated on other farms in the area, all in the same state of stasis. Dick and Joan Roberson's fields of organic garlic are covered in snow, as are Jeff and Jeanette Herman's Cliffside Orchards and Stephan Schott's beehives. The unionized employees of Schott's Mingo Mountain Apiary are tucked away in their waxy cells, waiting until the sun warms their wings and grows their food. The trees in John and Janet Crandall's Riverview Orchard a few miles away are bare, but the orchard's other business, Crandall Coffee Roasters, is busy in winter, roasting beans and delivering them to cafes in nearby towns. A rich, smoky aroma floats over their frozen fields near their farm, a pungent reminder that the industrious farmers in this area must find creative ways to supplement their seasonal farming income.

THE WORK OF THE SOIL, THE WORK OF THE HOUSE

Below ground, even during this freeze, the soil is at work. Dig into it and in the rich tilth deeper down you can feel life and even warmth. The word *tilth* itself comes from the Middle English *tilian* ("to till" or "to labor"), and this soil is definitely laboring—its microbes working away, completing the seasonal cycle of their development (see the sidebar "The Importance of Soil" by Shepherd's Grain farmers Fred Fleming and Karl Kupers later in this chapter). The rich browns and blacks of the compost pile are a stark contrast to all the white, and here is where the most activity is going on. Turn over a shovelful of earth: the steam rises—the soil is busier than the bees at this time of year, continuing to build itself.

Down the hill, inside the bunkhouse, it is a time of restoration, of dreaming and planning. As we enter the warm kitchen, the cold, clear, slightly smoky scent of the outside air is replaced with a range of smells—the meaty smokiness radiating all the way from the back room, where sausages and other cured meats are hanging on strings from a metal rack. Lora Lea is there and says, "Oh, you have to come and see the prosciutto." On the way through the bunkhouse, the smell of wood smoke from the stove mingles with the dusty, sunny aromas of the last of the season's tomatoes—picked from the vines green before the first freeze, now in various shades of pink and red, piled in baskets to slowly ripen. Lora Lea picks one up. "This is an Oxheart, see?" Yes, it has a pointed end, and it does resemble a heart—not a stylized valentine heart, but a real, bloody human heart.

That is how things are here, even in the quietest season—nothing is created just for show. This is a working farm, and the beauty around us is the authentic product of the work that is done. The back room is full of the season's final, quirky beauty—huge, knobby green squash, dozens of cobs of bright red corn peppered with deep purple kernels, hanging on their brittle stalks to dry. The riot of color is a contrast to the gentle greyness of the outside landscape. Here it is all about preserving the last of the harvest, extending its energies as long as possible.

Lora Lea and Rick shell dried Oaxacan Green Dent corn. Flour corn is one of the easiest grains to grow, harvest, and process by hand.

SEEDS OF CHANGE: PLANNING THE GARDEN

The long table in the kitchen, which in summer is packed with students and chefs eating and sharing conviviality, sits empty now but for six or seven bowls full of dried and drying corn and beans. And here, again, an explosion of color. Lora Lea lines them up on the table from darkest to lightest. On the end is the tiny matte black garbanzo, then the small glossy black Cherokee Trail of Tears, the larger, deep-maroon Vermont True Cranberry, and the tiny two-toned black-eyed pea that was sent to her by the Renewing America's Food Traditions (RAFT) project, which in its first year delivered seeds from about twenty endangered and indigenous plants to farmers and gardeners across the country for them to plant and share. The RAFT project hopes to increase diversity and preserve disappearing species native to each region (for more about this project, see the "Fall Preservation" chapter). Lora Lea received about a dozen seeds in 2005—her first year working with the group—and participated in a harvest dinner later that year during which the produce from those seeds was celebrated.

The next bean sorted on the kitchen table is the gorgeous Goat's Eye, with its dark-brown swirls around a tan center. The ocher Arikara Yellow (another RAFT bean) follows, then the beautiful Mayflower bean, with its cabernet-colored dusting on a creamy background. This latter bean was first brought to North America on the *Mayflower* in 1620. Next, the Tierra del Fuego shell bean is like the Goat's Eye but smaller and rounder, with swirls of deep red on a cream base. And the Jacob's Cattle bean, also known as the Trout bean, looks like a tiny Ayrshire cowhide with its deep red on white. The Hadatza Shield bean from South Dakota looks as though it has been dipped in white chocolate; the undercoat

Lora Lea uses a block of wood to clean Arabian Purple hulless barley, grown from rare seed obtained through Seed Savers Exchange.

is a minuscule fireworks display of red against pale tan. And last—but of course not least—is the reliable Lazy Housewife stringless, a pure, creamy white bean with a curvy kidney shape.

The colors, shapes, and names of these beans are fascinating; it is tempting to study each one as if it is a jewel. And in a sense they all are. They are the tiny gems stuffed with instructions, a map to find a treasure, if you will—and the treasure? More beans! Food, soup, sustenance. But to preserve and increase this wondrous diversity of form—and, one can only imagine, taste—this treasure map must be buried. As in the biblical parable of the talents, it must also be used and shared to increase in number. Think about how few particular breeds or types of food are available on the general market (and yet how many processed food products fill the shelves), then look at the abundance of diversity here—it is an incredible contrast! According to the Slow Food Terra Madre publication *Manifestos on the Future of Food and Seed*, of the "80,000 edible plants used for food, only about 150 of them are being cultivated, and just eight are traded globally." Some plants have been brought back from the brink of extinction through the efforts of just one farm.

Winter is a time to examine your beans—and it takes time. "I get so excited when I start thinking about what we will plant next season," says Lora Lea. "When I get those catalogs, I start dreaming." She orders her seeds from a few companies that feature non-GMO (genetically modified organism) heirloom varieties, and she follows the "Safe Seed Pledge" (see "Rethinking the Kitchen"), which stresses the risks of genetically engineered seeds. That pledge, envisioned and written by the Council for Responsible Genetics, has been signed by about eighty seed companies (and the number is growing) in the United States, Canada, and France, such as Territorial Seed Company in Oregon and Johnny's Selected Seeds in Maine, among other well-known and lesser-known companies. (In recent years Monsanto, the huge chemical and seed

Preserved salami and dry cured hams age in the cool winter air of the farm school.

company, has been acquiring small seed companies, and it is important for small, sustainable farms to continually research the source and production practices of the seeds they sow.)

Lora Lea buys her seeds from companies that follow the pledge, and she's also dedicated to seed saving and sharing with friends, neighbors, and fellow farmers. When she orders seeds, it's a several-day affair—going through catalogs, taking stock of what she already has, deciding what worked and what didn't, and looking for new vegetables, fruits, and other produce that she might want to plant.

AN EXTENDED COMMUNITY: A WEB OF INFORMATION

No farm can exist without the community that surrounds and supports it. In the case of Quillisascut Farm, the network reaches from this small piece of land in eastern Washington to the local grange in Rice, the nearby farms and towns of Colville and Kettle Falls, the larger city of Spokane, and most significantly to Seattle, where a whole community of chefs and food lovers are connected by their experiences at Quillisascut. The dynamic, enthusiastic young chefs who've spent time at the farm become a support network for other local farms, ranches, and even fishing boats as they return to Seattle deeply committed to featuring local, sustainably grown or sustainably harvested products on their menus: fish, meat, poultry, vegetables, fruits, nuts, and cheeses from Quillisascut and other local producers.

So Seattle is a large part of this story. When they first started making cheese, Rick and Lora Lea would hand-deliver their products to restaurants, creating a bond with the chefs they met. But, like most farmers, they can't visit the city often, especially in the height of summer when they are at their busiest. So now the chefs come to them. During the long cold months, however, Rick and Lora Lea have a little more time

Winter is a time to reconnect with friends. A few members of Slow Food Upper Columbia enjoy an evening of dinnertime conversation and good company (left to right: Don Worley, Jay Berube, Janice Berube, Lora Lea, and Rick).

on their hands. This time of year they travel to Seattle, Spokane, and the smaller communities near them to meet with like-minded chefs, friends, and colleagues who support sustainable farming.

Several organizations the Misterlys are members of—Chefs Collaborative, Rural Roots, Seed Savers Exchange, Slow Food, Tilth Producers, and Washington Sustainable Food and Farming Network—host activities, dinners, and workshops where members can exchange information. Other events are just informal gatherings of attuned citizens who get together and share stories, seeds, and harvests. One notable event in 2002 was a goat-cheese tasting, which brought together goat-cheese producers from across Washington to share their cheese and

stories with Slow Food members. Lora Lea brought a slide show of her goats—Chickpea, Myrtle, Sally, Spotty Lou, Sterling, and the rest of the girls—so the group could "meet the producers." The cheese lovers were captivated; it was at this meeting that many local chefs learned about Quillisascut Farm, passing information on to others in various organizations.

Most of the chefs who regularly visit the farm came to it through their association with the Seattle chapter of Chefs Collaborative (see "Rethinking the Kitchen"), a nonprofit organization with a national membership that focuses on promoting sustainable practices in the professional kitchen. For several years the organization was known by the amusing acronym FORKS (Fields, Oceans, Ranches, Kitchens, Stewards). The chefs who visit the farm are students at community

college programs or working chefs cooking at some of Seattle's top restaurants. In past years Kurt Beecher Dammeier, owner of Beecher's Handmade Cheese in Seattle's Pike Place Market, has thrown an annual Quillisascut kickoff party at his cheese shop.

Since 2002, the Seattle chapter of Chefs Collaborative has sponsored a scholarship that pays for one student chef each summer to attend a session at Quillisascut. Chef Christopher Conville, former executive director of the Seattle Art Museum's Taste restaurant, and the restaurant's general manager, Danielle Custer, both received scholarships through Chefs Collaborative to attend the school. They left the farm changed by the experience and even more dedicated to sourcing local produce, fish, meat, and wine for the restaurant. "At Taste, we try to source foods from as many local farms as we can and educate our diners about sustain-

A still-damp kid snuggles with her mother after the hard work of being born.

The Importance of Soil
by Fred Fleming and Karl Kupers, Shepherd's Grain

At Shepherd's Grain, an eastern Washington wheat-farming cooperative, we produce grains from an alliance of progressive family farms dedicated to practicing sustainable agriculture. Our farming practices have been certified "environmentally and socially responsible" by Food Alliance. We produce high-quality products from the crops we raise. This way you get the best nutritional benefits. We are also new members of the Whole Grains Council.

We talk a lot about tillage erosion, which occurs each and every time you till the soil, but water erosion is the most visible and therefore the most dramatic. The many freeze-and-thaw cycles, along with numerous rains and snowfalls, have created a serious impact on the tillage-based soils of the Northwest. Soil erodes down newly formed gullies, literally slides off hills, and overflows onto roadways once the ditch banks are full. Once you have made the commitment to change that impact by becoming a direct seeder (sowing seeds into the soil without plowing or disturbing the previous year's grain stubble), watching soil erosion produces a greater sense of despair than before. It's hard to overemphasize how significant that concern is in a wheat producer's mind. Direct seeding is all about the soil, its health, its microbial populations, and its water-holding capacity—its ability to produce a healthy crop. Erosion of all kinds defeats those efforts. This erosion of the soil impacts the local county road crew's budget, the fish in the streams and eventually in the rivers of the Northwest, the need to dredge the Columbia River mouth for ship access to Portland, the ability to have productive soils left for the next generation to create renewable fuels—and the list can go on and on.

---

ability," says Conville. "At Quillisascut, we had the chance to make a stronger connection between the foods on the plate and the farm, [and] how much work actually goes into producing these foods." Conville and Custer believe that this type of connection is important not only to their profession but also to the home cook who is looking for ideas or new sources for products.

And, indeed, the lettuce in the salad (from Full Circle Farm) or the beef tenderloin (from Skagit River Ranch) at Taste often can also be found at local farmers markets. Chefs Collaborative and chefs like Conville help close the circle between the farmer and the chef or the home cook by creating a network of information and a love of good, fresh food.

KIDDING!
A NEW GENERATION EMERGES

As winter softens, precipitation turns from snow to sleet to drizzle and rain and then to more clear days. Even the goats feel it coming. In February, Lora Lea writes in her winter diary:

This morning we woke up to a couple inches of new snow. Yesterday's dreams were warming up and pointing to spring, marveling over the daffodils and tulips pushing out of the ground, a feather of bronze fennel poking up, gathering flats for starting seeds, and getting ready for baby goats to arrive. But today there is a chill and I want to revert to my favorite winter activity of late, which is huddling by the fire with a cup of steaming tea, lost in a good book.

The reality is that life on the farm is gearing up for the new season. The first goat kids of the year arrived on Thursday—Pansy

Chef Profile: Thierry Rautureau
Rover's, Seattle, Washington

Born in a small village in Brittany in northwestern France, Thierry Rautureau has made his career in the United States, with the famous Rover's restaurant in Seattle's upscale Madison Valley neighborhood, where he has gained "best restaurant" awards year after year from numerous publications. But Rautureau's true passion is not success, it is taste—and community. He was one of the first major chefs to come to Quillisascut, and from the very beginning he has supported the farm by offering Quillisascut cheeses on his menu.

"In 1988, Lora Lea walked up to the back door of my kitchen with a wonderful flat-weave basket filled with her goat's milk cheeses," says Rautureau. "I looked at her and said, 'Where have you been all my life?'" He laughs, remembering that local farmers were one big reason he came to Seattle. "Pike Place Market is a great place," he says.

One Labor Day weekend he visited the farm, where he had a great experience cooking and eating with the Misterlys and a few other guests. Lora Lea asked him,

"Do you think chefs would be interested in coming out here?" Rautureau encouraged them to set up the school. The first young chefs who came to the farm and had a passion for its products were all infected with Thierry's enthusiasm for fresh, local, artisan products like the ones he had grown up with in France. When he came to the farm himself, he worked hard (even though he didn't have to) and played with the ingredients, just as his sous-chefs were to do later.

As a boy Rautureau worked, along with his brother and sister, on his grandparents' small wheat farm connected to a local castle. His grandparents also had cows, ducks, chickens, and a garden, and it was they who instilled in him a love for farming, a connection to the land, and a respect for gathering and preserving the bounties of the local landscape. As Lora Lea says, "We have seen him pass on his love for and commitment to local quality products and the relationships he has built over the years to all who pass through his kitchen and his restaurant."

had triplet boys. She is our indicator that we have a few days and then bam! *off and running with kids everywhere, new milk, new cheese—and spring around the bend.*

So instead of sitting by the fire, Rick is cleaning the barn and getting all the birthing stalls spic and span and laid out with a blanket of fresh straw. I filled the trays with compost and seed-starting medium and planted onion seeds: Gold Coin, Red Marble (cipollini), Mars (a large red slicer), Prince (good for storage), Ailsa Craig (early large sweet onion), and King Richard leeks. As soon as the other seeds arrive, I will plant a few more varieties: the Blue Solaize

leek (it sounds like a song and looks so beautiful in the garden) and the Laura leek (I can't resist!).

A BROADER VISION

Dreaming and planning in winter about how the farm will develop in spring wouldn't be complete without thinking about the future of the food system itself. Living on a working farm, Lora Lea and Rick must conserve where they can, but this way of thinking is also a way of life that is of vital importance. Especially in winter, when the holidays provide hope for creating a world where all have access to clean water, air, land, and healthy food, we realize how our food or household-purchasing choices impact our communities, the larger food system, and even other natural systems that are contributing to global climate change.

Some of the most basic concepts that the Quillisascut Farm School is committed to are some of the easiest: purchasing only what is needed, so foods won't spoil; buying organic products from local farms; walking or taking the bus to local farmers markets; cutting back on purchases of consumer items; sharing with family and friends or buying used items; and even just turning off the lights when leaving a room. The silence and beauty of the winter season brings with it our collective dream for peace on Earth, that through local actions toward community prosperity, peaceful farming practices, and thoughtful earth-friendly actions, we are taking steps to heal our communities and making broader change possible. In these and other ways we may even find it possible to design a global community that values and protects all that the earth offers.

THE HISTORY OF QUILLISASCUT FARM

Lora Lea was raised on a farm in Leavenworth, Washington, where her family had a small dairy and her mother made farm-style cheese and butter from the summer milk surplus. "I remember the taste of fresh curds, real creamed cottage cheese and butter," says Lora Lea. "It's a taste that isn't duplicated in anything found at the local grocer. Cheesemaking seemed a natural part of my life as a child. It is familiar, and I loved staying home and making a living with our animals."

That cheese was the inspiration behind the cheese now being made at Quillisascut Farm. Rick and Lora Lea bought twenty-six acres in 1981 and began making cheese for home use that year (in 1994 they bought an additional ten acres). In 1985 they began to seriously consider starting a cheese business, and Lora Lea took a four-day cheesemaking course at Washington State University. "It opened my eyes to a whole new level in the

world of cheese," she says. They received their license from the Washington Department of Agriculture to produce raw milk cheese in 1987. Today the Misterlys milk about forty goats twice a day, about ten months of the year (except for a month or so in winter, when the goats give very little milk and many of them are getting ready to have their kids).

Snowball and the girls, inside the steamy barn waiting for a dinner of alfalfa hay

Lora Lea's Seed List

Each year in February, Lora Lea orders seeds from catalogs for the coming year to supplement the seeds she has saved from the year before. This list is extensive, made up of old heirloom varieties and hardy standbys as well as new seeds that she thinks might do well in the garden. She tries to have a wide range of vegetables, fruits, berries, nuts, and flowers in the garden and orchard to help bolster the biodiversity on the farm. This also creates a wide range of sources for pollinators—bees, butterflies, hummingbirds, and other birds and insects—to visit.

Johnny's Selected Seeds

Beans: Flagrano (French flageolet), Gentec 401 (cannellini), Provider, Red Noodle, Tavera

Beets: Chioggia, golden

Brussels sprouts: Oliver

Cabbage: Primax, Red Express

Carrots: Rainbow

Celeriac: Diamant

Corn: Spring Treat

Cucumber: Tasty Jade

Eggplant: Beatrice, Fairy Tale

Fennel: Zefa Fino (bulb fennel)

Kohlrabi: Eder

Okra: Cajun Delight

Onions: Copra, King Richard leek, Mars, Red Marble

Parsnip: Lancer

Peas: Caselode, Dwarf Grey (for flowers and tendrils), sugar snap

Soybean: Envy

Summer squash: Raven (F1), Sebring (F1)

Sweet potato: Beauregard

Flowers: Benary's Giant Mix zinnia, Bombay Fire (celosia), Love-Lies-Bleeding (amaranth)

Herbs: Sorrel, minutina (Herba Stella)

Seed Savers Exchange

Beans: Runner cannellini

Cabbage: Premium Late Flat Dutch

Carrots: Dragon, Oxheart

Cucumber: Parisian Pickling

Leeks: Blue Solaize

Lettuce: Merveille des Quatre Saisons

Melons: Blacktail Mountain watermelon, Emerald Gem, Noir des Carmes

Peppers: Ancho Gigantea, Chervena Chushka

Tomatoes: Isis Candy (cherry)

Flowers: California poppy mixture, Chinese aster 'Matsumoto' mixture, lupine 'Tall Russell,' morning glory 'White Cypress Vine,' salpiglossis 'Painted Tongue,' petunia 'Old Fashioned Vining,' sunflower 'Titan,' zinnia 'Benary's Giant'

Nichols Seed Company

Pepper: Pimiento de Padrón

Rutabaga: Purple Top Yellow

Flowers: Kiss Me Over the Garden Gate; morning glory 'Cypress Vine,' 'Grandpa Ott's,' 'Moonflower'; ornamental millet F1 'Purple Majesty'; nasturtium 'Tall Single mixture'; Nicotiana sylvestris; sweet pea 'Grandiflora Old Spice mixture'; Verbena bonariensis; zinnia 'Envy'

Herb: Sorrel 'Blood Veined'

"I was twenty-five years old and Rick was twenty-eight when we bought this land," Lora Lea says. "But the direction our farm would take was more like a seed that we carried, and when we planted it, we didn't know what it would look like." When they moved to their new land, they brought with them a milking Alpine doe named Taffy, her month-old daughter named Sasha, and two week-old kids, Weenza and Artie, from Lora Lea's mother's goat. Since the farm didn't have any electricity yet, Lora Lea and Rick would set the milk to make a soft cheese in their outdoor kitchen. Then they would store it in a sealed plastic bucket and drop it from a rope down into the well, where it would stay cool while the summer temperatures soared into the 90s. "The process of turning milk into cheese is really simple and captivating," says Lora Lea. "We tried to make all of our own food, and it was fun to experiment with new recipes to make different types of cheese. It was a hobby that really took off."

Today, two decades later, the Misterlys sell their cheeses at some of the best specialty food shops and restaurants in Seattle. "Our dream has always been a holistic one of an integrated farm. I try to look at our farm as a work in progress with many different parts," Lora Lea says. While others might see it simply as a goat cheese farm, this, like so many other small farms, is as much a process as a place, coming from humble beginnings and growing to become the center of a community.

Lora Lea cuts the curds in the morning's set of cheese while the previous day's cheese dries on racks before being moved into the aging room.

The Challenges of Sustainable Cooking in Winter
by Norman Six, Lovitt Restaurant, Colville, Washington

Winter presents a serious challenge to a small restaurant like Lovitt. Luckily, a great deal of human history was spent working out techniques to conquer this most inhospitable season. The techniques we use regularly are canning, freezing, drying—and compromise.

For a restaurant, canning in wide-mouth Mason Ball jars is a formidable task, so it is good to remember that all those late nights spent canning during harvest enable almost effortless desserts and side dishes in winter. We buy fruit when it's at its best and cheapest and so bursting ripe that it can't go to market. We can those ripe peaches and other fruits in honey water, and in February they really do taste like August sunshine. Jarred fruit is beautiful as well: Using jars as decoration around the restaurant is a casual way of letting guests know how seriously we take our product sourcing.

Staying local year-round requires not only dedication and education but also a lot of space—space for freezers and refrigerators, cool dry rooms, and cool humid rooms. This need for varied storage environments was the main reason we located our restaurant on an 1890s farm. The massive root cellar lets us keep roots, bulbs, and gourds for months without artificial cooling or humidity control. This is both our simplest and our cheapest preservation technique: stack the squash in October, cook it in March.

We do freeze a lot of berries, vegetables, mushrooms, and sauces, but the main reason we keep several large freezers is for the meat. Dealing directly with small farms means buying whole animals at the right time—not just chickens and rabbits but a whole steer and a few hogs or turkeys at a time. So we have to have a very flexible menu and a flexible clientele. Our customers understand that if we run out of frozen chicken in January, there won't be any more until June.

When good planning and estimating fail us, compromise is in order. We source our seafood regionally rather than locally. This means that as winter drags on and we are running out of chicken or pork, we can add a second seafood entrée. Winter is also a great time to use the tropical fruits—like bananas, pineapples, and coconuts—that have been part of winter diets of Northern Europeans and Americans for centuries. These fruits are suited to long, slow shipping, so they don't need to be flown in. And, best of all, they don't undermine any local producers.

The thing we find most surprising about running a local seasonal restaurant is how, once the techniques and the timing are learned, it's not a lot more challenging than running a traditional fine-dining restaurant. It is also a pleasantly humbling experience. Instead of demanding whatever ingredients you need to create the menu you envision, you create by using what the local growers provide. In our restaurant local procurement drives creativity, rather than creativity driving procurement.

Rick and herding collie Jet walk past the farm school building on their way to feed goats and cows in the lower pasture of the farm.

WINTER
RECIPES

WINTER IN OUR FARM KITCHEN has us turning the oven down for long, slow braises; we are raiding the larder for dried beans and grains for warming stews. We are rationing our precious jars of preserves and dried fruits that we put up in summer. We don't feel lacking though, as apples abound and sweet roots like parsnips, rutabagas, and onions are plentiful. Aged cheeses, cured meats, and crisp pickles invite us to the table. Our work is finishing the butchering for the season; curing ham, breasola, bacon; and stuffing sausage. An occasional wild game offering keeps things interesting.

BREAKFAST & BREADS

Cardamom–Apple Stuffed French Toast with Cider Syrup
MAKES 4 SERVINGS

I use hominy bread (a yeasted bread made with a mixture of wheat flour and corn flour) for this recipe; its slightly nutty flavor prevents the dish from being too sweet. If you can't find it in your local market, a good sourdough works well. Adding the sugar to the apples at the beginning of the cooking process keeps them firmer. For a lower-fat version, milk or half-and-half may be substituted for the heavy cream.

Preheat the oven to 200 degrees F.

French toast:
4 Honeycrisp (or other tart) apples, cored, quartered, and cut into ¼-inch-thick slices
4 tablespoons organic sugar (evaporated cane juice)
1 teaspoon ground cardamom

A good way to use apples that are soft from storage is to cook them in recipes like Cardamom–Apple Stuffed French Toast.

4 tablespoons (½ stick) unsalted butter, divided
4 eggs
½ cup heavy cream
¼ teaspoon vanilla
Pinch of kosher salt
4 slices hominy bread, cut 1½ inches thick

Cider syrup:
1 cup apple cider
1 cup organic sugar (evaporated cane juice)

In a small bowl, toss the apples with sugar and cardamom. In a sauté pan over medium-high heat, melt 2 tablespoons of the butter. Add the apples and stir occasionally for about 3 minutes, or until the apples are soft and lightly browned. Remove from heat and cool slightly in the pan.

Meanwhile, in a small bowl, whisk together the eggs, heavy cream, vanilla, and salt until frothy. Slice a long slit in each piece of the hominy bread from the top crust to about an inch from the bottom and side crusts. Stuff the bread with the apples; reserve a few apples to garnish the dish. Pour the egg–cream mixture onto a plate and soak the stuffed bread in batches, turning until saturated.

Melt 1 tablespoon of the butter in a large sauté pan over medium-high heat. Place two slices of the bread in the pan and cook until brown, about 2 minutes on each side. Remove from the pan and keep warm in a 200-degree oven. Repeat with the remaining 2 slices of bread and butter.

To prepare the cider syrup, pour the apple cider and sugar into a small saucepan. Bring to a boil, then reduce the liquid to 1 cup. Serve the French toast warm with butter, the reserved apples, and cider syrup.

Method Cooking in a Seasonal Kitchen
by Chef Kären Jurgensen, Quillisascut Farm School of the Domestic Arts

At the Quillisascut Farm School "eating local" is a key principle. In my classes I teach cooks how to develop recipes around ingredients (veggies, grains, meat, dairy, eggs, nuts, and so on) that are in season, as well as how to preserve and save them for winter. Learning "method cooking" or cooking "techniques" allows for more flexibility in a seasonal kitchen. This way a cook is inspired by ingredients as they come into season, rather than being tied to a specific recipe. Being versed in the methods of steaming, braising, roasting, and so on lets the cook adapt recipes quickly and easily, and it also fosters a creative spirit.

In the recipes included throughout this book we have specified the exact name of each ingredient we use on the farm, but you can substitute ingredients that might be easier to find, as well as fresh, locally grown produce from your local farmers market. For instance, we used Vermont True Cranberry beans for the egg dish (see the recipe in this chapter for Vermont True Cranberry Beans and Poached Araucana Eggs), but many other hearty beans would also work. The eggs used in the same dish came from our own Araucana chickens here on the farm, but your market's cage-free eggs will work just as well. Enjoy the names of our original ingredients as you peruse the recipes, but certainly use what works for you.

We hope you'll view these recipes as a gift between friends, similar to a treasured recipe passed down by your grandmother.

Seasonal variations: Peaches, plums, apricots, or pears may be substituted for the apples. Similarly, the juice of these fruits may be substituted for the apple cider in the syrup.

Toasted Oatmeal, Rolled Spelt, and Chamomile
MAKES 2 SERVINGS

Rolled spelt is chewier in texture than the oatmeal you may know. The chamomile adds a subtle sweet note without adding sugar. Dried chamomile blossoms are available in the bulk tea section of your grocery store or from your local herbalist.

2 tablespoons (¼ stick) unsalted butter

¾ cup rolled oats

¾ cup rolled spelt

2 tablespoons dried chamomile blossoms

¼ cup heavy cream

1½ cup goat's milk (or cow's milk),
    plus additional milk for serving

Pinch of salt

Brown sugar (optional)

Chopped walnuts (optional)

Melt the butter in a large saucepan over medium heat. Add the oats, spelt, and chamomile blossoms. Cook for a few minutes, stirring until the oats start to turn toasty brown. Pour in the heavy cream, tossing to coat, and cook for 1 minute more. Add the goat's milk and cook until the milk is absorbed. Season with salt to taste.

Divide the mixture into two bowls. Serve with milk and top with brown sugar and chopped walnuts if desired.

Variations: Top oatmeal with sautéed apples, pears, or poached fruits and toasted hazelnuts. Substitute anise seed for chamomile blossoms, top with stewed cherries.

Vermont True Cranberry Beans and Poached Araucana Eggs with Chipotle Sauce
MAKES 4 SERVINGS

This recipe is a winter morning warm-up but could be a nutritious light supper as well. The rich egg yolks, cheese, and

Starting the day with a hearty winter meal of beans and eggs topped with chipotle sauce fuels the body and warms the palate.

Quark—a German-style cultured milk product similar to plain yogurt or sour cream, available in many grocery stores—cool your mouth in contrast to the spicy beans and smoky sauce. Pinto beans, Anasazi beans, black beans, or other dried beans can be substituted; cooking times will vary. The older the beans, the longer the cooking time. The beans can be cooked up to 3 days ahead and reheated gently.

Note: If dried beans are cooked on anything above a simmer, the result will be popped skins and mushy beans. Always keep the liquid level above the beans to prevent broken skins. Also, canned beans are not a suitable substitute as the beans make their own stock and sauce.

Beans:

> 1½ cups (about ½ pound) Vermont True Cranberry
> beans, rinsed and soaked overnight (3 parts water to 1
> part beans, soaking water reserved)
>
> 2 teaspoons kosher salt
>
> 4 cloves garlic, finely chopped
>
> ½ cup diced yellow onion
>
> 2 to 3 dried arbol chiles (optional)
>
> 1 dried bay leaf
>
> 8 to 10 whole black peppercorns
>
> 1 teaspoon ground cumin

Chipotle sauce:

> 1 dozen dried chipotle chiles, stemmed and seeded
>
> ¾ cup boiling water
>
> Pinch of kosher salt

Eggs:

> 2 teaspoons kosher salt
>
> 8 Araucana eggs (or other eggs)
>
> ½ cup (about 2 ounces) shredded goat cheese
> (or Cheddar cheese)
>
> 4 tablespoons Quark or plain yogurt

In a 2-quart stockpot over medium-high heat, bring the beans and soaking water to a boil, then skim foam from the beans. Reduce heat to a simmer. Add the salt, garlic, onion, chiles, bay leaf, and black peppercorns. Simmer gently about 45 minutes, uncovered, or until the beans are soft with a buttery texture and flavor (add water if necessary). Add the cumin and adjust salt if necessary. Discard the bay leaf.

To prepare the chipotle sauce, toast the chiles in a dry saucepan over medium heat, until the skins start to change color but not burn. Remove from heat and cover with the boiling water. Allow to steep for 15 minutes. Remove the chiles from water (reserve water) and put them in a mortar or small food processor. Grind the chiles, slowly adding water, working to a smooth paste and then to a thick sauce. Strain through a medium sieve. Stir in the salt. The sauce is very spicy hot—use sparingly. It can be made ahead and stored in an airtight container in the refrigerator for up to 2 weeks.

To poach the eggs, bring 2 quarts water to a simmer in a medium saucepan and add salt. Gently break the eggs into a small ramekin and slip them, one by one, into the water. Cover the pan and turn off the heat. Steep gently until the whites are just set and the yolk is soft (about 2½ minutes, depending on the size of the egg). Remove the eggs with a slotted spoon.

To assemble the dish, divide the beans among 4 bowls, top each with 2 poached eggs. Divide the goat cheese evenly among the bowls, top with 1 tablespoon of Quark, and drizzle with the chipotle sauce. Serve immediately.

Seasonal variations: In summer use a fresh tomato salsa or pico de gallo and fresh cilantro for toppings in place of the chipotle sauce. Adding acid to the beans will affect the texture and cooking time; if you use tomatoes, add them after the beans are soft.

SOUPS & SALADS

Jacob's Cattle Bean, Kale, and Chèvre Soup
MAKES 8 SERVINGS

The goat cheese adds a delicious tang to this comforting soup. The heavy cream binds the beans together and makes the soup thicker, so resist the urge to substitute whole milk or half-and-half. Because of the heavy fat content, this soup freezes well.

Note: Canned beans are not a suitable substitute as the beans make their own stock.

Jacob's Cattle beans

2 cups (about 12 ounces) Jacob's Cattle beans or other white beans, rinsed and soaked overnight (3 parts water to 1 part beans, soaking water reserved)

2 tablespoons salt

2 tablespoons (¼ stick) unsalted butter

1 medium carrot, diced

1 celery stalk, diced

1 medium yellow onion, diced

2 cloves garlic, finely chopped

1½ cups tomato purée

1 cup chopped preserved or purchased roasted red peppers

1 bunch black kale (or other kale), about 8 to 10 leaves, stemmed and chopped

2 dried bay leaves

1 tablespoon dried thyme

1 teaspoon red chili flakes

1 cup heavy cream

1½ cups (about ¾ pound) soft goat cheese

1 teaspoon freshly ground black pepper

Kosher salt

Put the beans and soaking water in a large stockpot over medium-high heat. Bring to a boil and skim foam from the beans. Reduce the heat to a gentle simmer and add the salt (the water should taste lightly of salt). Cook about 1 hour, until the beans are soft in texture and creamy in flavor.

In another saucepan, melt the butter over medium heat, add the carrot, celery, yellow onion, and garlic, and cook until the mixture is soft but not brown. Stir in the tomato purée, red peppers, and black kale. Cook for 4 to 5 minutes and add salt to taste.

When the beans have finished cooking, stir in the vegetable mixture, bay leaves, thyme, and chili flakes. Cook for about 20 minutes, then add the heavy cream, goat cheese, and black pepper. Cook for 15 minutes more, then season to taste with salt.

Friends from the area prepare to dine on homemade sausages and braised cabbage.

Variations: In summer use fresh tomatoes, peppers, and thyme. For a lighter minestrone-style soup, leave out the heavy cream and goat cheese.

ENTRÉES

Lamb–Potato Sausages with Braised Cabbage, Chiles, and Apples
MAKES 6 SERVINGS

This is an easy treatment for cabbage—the apples, chiles, and apple cider brighten the dish and keep it from feeling too heavy. If you don't want to make your own lamb–potato sausage, you may substitute any sausage patty or link.

2 tablespoons (¼ stick) unsalted butter

½ yellow onion, cut into thin strips from bulb
    to blossom end

5 cloves garlic, whole

1 small head Savoy cabbage, cored and sliced

2 Cameo apples (or other), cored and sliced

2 dried arbol chiles

6 to 8 whole black peppercorns

1 tablespoon mild-flavored honey, such as clover
    or fireweed

2 cups apple cider

2 tablespoons cider vinegar

Kosher salt

Oil or bacon fat for frying

1½ pounds Lamb–Potato Sausage (recipe follows in the
    "Winter Pantry" section), formed into 4 patties

Melt the butter in a braising pan over medium heat. Add the onion and garlic and cook for 3 to 4 minutes. Stir in the cabbage and apples, cook for a few minutes, then add the chiles, peppercorns, and honey. Pour in the apple cider, reduce the heat to medium low, and cover. Cook for another 10 minutes, until cabbage is wilted.

Uncover the pan and turn the heat up to medium-high. Cook the cabbage mixture, stirring occasionally, until most of the liquid is gone. Add the cider vinegar and season with salt to taste. Continue cooking until all liquid is gone.

While the cabbage is braising, heat a bit of oil in a cast iron or other heavy skillet over medium heat, until the oil slides easily in the pan. Fry the lamb–potato sausage patties for 3 to 5 minutes on each side. Serve with the cabbage and its pan juices.

Curried Lamb Stew with Farro, Filberts, and Dried Plums

MAKES 6 SERVINGS

Farro is an ancient whole grain, a predecessor to wheat, full of nutrients. It is available at most specialty food stores, but you can substitute wheat berries if you can't find it. This recipe plays with texture: softly stewed vegetables, toothy grain, and the crunch of filberts make the dish interesting. Using dried fruits in winter reminds us of the summer's bounty and adds a natural sweetness to this dish.

Note: Store-bought stock contains high amounts of sodium; if you are not using homemade stock in this recipe, be sure to adjust the salt accordingly.

Lamb stew:

3½ pounds lamb leg meat or stew meat, cut into
    1½-inch cubes

1½ tablespoons salt

½ teaspoon freshly ground black pepper

2 tablespoons oil or lard

1½ tablespoons Madras curry powder

1 medium yellow onion, chopped roughly into 1-inch
    pieces

3 cloves garlic, thinly sliced

1 medium carrot, peeled and chopped

2 parsnips, peeled and chopped

4 cups lamb, veal, or chicken stock

1 cup pitted dried plums, whole

Farro:

¾ cup whole filberts

6 cups chicken or vegetable stock

1 tablespoon kosher salt

3 cups farro (soaked for 1 hour and rinsed)

3 tablespoons minced chives, plus 2 tablespoons
    for garnish
1 tablespoon chopped fresh thyme

Season the lamb meat with salt and pepper. Heat the oil in a medium braising pan until it slides easily across the pan. Brown the lamb on all sides.

Add the curry powder, onion, and garlic to the braising pan. Cook and stir for a few minutes, then add the carrots, parsnips, and stock. The stock should cover the lamb (add water if needed). Cook, covered, over low heat (a slow simmer) for 1 hour; you may also cook in a 300-degree oven for 1 hour.

Add the plums to the braising pan. Continue to cook partially covered until the lamb is fork tender, about 1 hour longer. Check liquid level occasionally to be certain that not too much is evaporating; add water or stock sparingly if needed. The liquid should reduce to a sauce consistency by the time the meat is done.

Chop the filberts roughly and toast in a frying pan over medium heat, until just fragrant and golden brown. Reserve.

To prepare the farro, put the farro, stock, and salt in a medium saucepan and bring to a simmer. Cook over medium-low heat until the farro is soft but a little chewy and the liquid is absorbed, 45 minutes to 1 hour. Add water or stock during cooking if necessary. Stir in the filberts, chives, and thyme. Season with salt to taste.

To assemble this dish, spoon the lamb stew over the farro and garnish with a sprinkle of chives. Serve immediately.

Variations: Dried apricots or dates with almonds or walnuts would be equally delicious in this recipe.

Oxtail and Parsnip Lasagne

MAKES ABOUT 12 SERVINGS

This rich and warming lasagne is a great way to use an uncommon cut of meat—the "whole beast" eating philosophy. It also shows off the underappreciated parsnip, which, when paired with freshly grated nutmeg, becomes glorious. This dish can be assembled up to 2 days ahead, then baked when ready to serve. Be sure to remove from the refrigerator 2 hours before baking for even cooking.

Oxtail sauce:
2 tablespoons olive oil
4½ pounds meaty oxtails, seasoned with salt and pepper
4 cloves garlic, whole
1 medium yellow onion, sliced
2 medium carrots, peeled and chopped
1 cup red wine
One 28-ounce can diced tomatoes, with liquid
1 cup veal (or other) stock or water
3 dried arbol chiles
2 dried bay leaves
1 dozen whole black peppercorns
¼ cup cognac

Parsnips:
4 cups (about 2½ pounds) peeled and sliced parsnips
2 tablespoons olive oil
Kosher salt

Lasagne:
1 pound fresh uncooked pasta sheets

Béchamel:
8 tablespoons (1 stick) unsalted butter
½ cup all-purpose flour

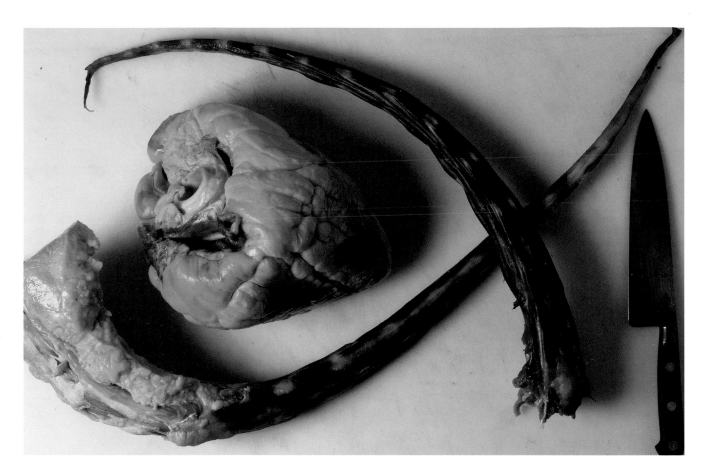

Oxtail and beef heart are foundations for rich tasting braises and important examples of using as much of the animal carcass as possible.

3 cups whole milk, scalded

1 teaspoon freshly grated nutmeg

¼ teaspoon freshly ground black pepper

Salt

1½ cups grated Gruyère (about 5 ounces) or other
    hard cheese

For the oxtail sauce:

Preheat the oven to 325 degrees F. Heat the olive oil in a large braising pan over high heat and season the oxtails with salt and pepper. Cook the oxtails until brown, turning on all sides. Add the garlic, onion, carrots, red wine, tomatoes, stock, arbol chiles, bay leaves, peppercorns, and cognac. Place covered pan in the oven and braise for 4 hours, or until meat pulls easily from the bone.

Remove from the oven and cool enough to pull meat from the bones and tear into small pieces. Discard bones. Put the meat back into the braising pan with the sauce and vegetables. Reduce liquid until thick but still saucy. Reserve.

For the parsnips:

Preheat the oven to 400 degrees F. In a mixing bowl, toss the parsnips in olive oil and salt. Spread them on a rimmed baking sheet, and roast in the oven for 14 minutes, or until golden. Remove from the oven and reserve. Lower the oven heat to 350 degrees F for baking the dish upon final assembly.

For the béchamel:

In a small saucepan, melt the butter over medium heat. Mix in the flour until smooth. Whisk in the scalded milk, and add the nutmeg and pepper. Season with salt. Cook over low heat until the flour taste is gone, about 40 minutes. Stir in the Gruyère. Reserve.

For the lasagne assembly:

In a 9 x 13-inch baking dish, layer the reserved parsnips, uncooked pasta sheets, and oxtail sauce, alternating layers until all of the ingredients are used, ending with a pasta layer. Top with the reserved béchamel. Bake for 45 minutes, or until golden and set. Let rest for 10 minutes before cutting.

Variations: Pork, lamb shoulder, or beef shank would also work in the braise. For a late-summer meal, use roasted eggplant and chiles in place of the parsnips.

Anise Seed Roast Pork with Celeriac Mash
MAKES 4 TO 6 SERVINGS

Celeriac, also known as celery root, is an often overlooked vegetable with a celery–parsley aroma, which adds complexity to this dish. I recommend using organic or pastured pork for better moisture and flavor. Garlic stored in winter will start to sprout a shoot in each clove, which can be bitter, so be sure to remove it. When boiling dense root vegetables like potatoes and celeriac, start the cooking process in cold water. This method allows the inside of the vegetable to cook without the outside turning to mush.

Roast pork:

    2 pounds pork loin
    5 cloves garlic, thinly sliced
    1 tablespoon anise seed, crushed lightly with mortar
        and pestle

    ½ tablespoon kosher salt
    ½ teaspoon freshly ground black pepper

Celeriac mash:

    1 pound celeriac, peeled and cut into 2-inch pieces
    3 russet potatoes (about 1 pound), peeled and
        cut into 2-inch pieces
    2 tablespoons (¼ stick) unsalted butter
    ¼ cup heavy cream or sour cream
    ¼ teaspoon freshly grated nutmeg
    Kosher salt

Preheat the oven to 400 degrees F.

Trim the pork loin of any silver skin but leave fat intact. With a sharp knife tip, shallowly score the loin on all sides. Slip the garlic into the scores. In a small bowl, combine the anise seed, salt, and pepper and rub the surface of the loin with the mixture.

Put the loin in a heavy cast iron skillet or roasting pan and cook in the preheated oven for 10 minutes. Reduce the heat to 350 degrees and continue cooking for 25 more minutes, or until the internal temperature reaches 155 degrees. Let the loin rest for about 7 minutes before slicing. Reserve pan juices to pour over when serving.

To prepare the celeriac mash, put the celeriac and potatoes into separate saucepans and cover with water. Bring each to a boil and cook until tender, about 15 minutes. Drain and run both vegetables through a food mill into a large bowl. Stir in the butter, heavy cream, and nutmeg. Season with salt to taste.

Variation: For more intense celeriac flavor, omit the potatoes; however, the purée will be somewhat looser.

DESSERTS

Coffee Toffee Bread Pudding with Cajeta Sauce
MAKES 8 SERVINGS

This recipe is a great way to use up leftover bread and brewed coffee. *Dulce de leche* (available in Latino markets) or caramel sauce can be substituted for *cajeta* sauce.

Celeriac is an under-used root vegetable that stores well for winter meals.

4 eggs

½ cup milk

½ cup heavy cream

½ cup organic sugar (evaporated cane juice)

½ teaspoon kosher salt

½ cup Cajeta Sauce (recipe follows in the "Winter Pantry" section), plus 1 cup for serving

½ cup strong brewed coffee or espresso, room temperature

1 pound brioche, challah, or other enriched yeast bread, cut into 1-inch cubes

Preheat the oven to 350 degrees F and butter a 9-inch round cake pan.

In a mixing bowl, whisk together the eggs, milk, heavy cream, sugar, and salt until a thick, custardlike consistency is reached. Pour half of the egg mixture into another bowl and whisk in ½ cup of the cajeta sauce. Whisk the coffee into the other bowl.

Divide the brioche into two bowls. Pour the coffee–custard mixture over one of the bowls and the cajeta–custard mixture over the other. Toss each thoroughly, until the brioche has absorbed all the liquid.

Spread the coffee brioche cubes into the bottom of the prepared cake pan and press lightly to close any gaps. Then layer the cajeta brioche cubes on top, again pressing lightly to close any gaps. Place in the center of the oven and bake, uncovered, for 40 minutes, or until the center is set. Let cool briefly in the pan before removing.

In a small saucepan, gently heat 1 cup cajeta sauce. Unmold the bread pudding, cut, and serve with heated cajeta sauce drizzled on top.

Walnut–Italian Plum Cake
MAKES 10 SERVINGS

This recipe comes from the pastry chef Lynda Oosterhuis, who graced the table at Quillisascut Farm with fresh baked breads and pastries from our outdoor brick oven for an entire summer. Lynda nurtured the animals and planted a grain garden for the students to understand different varieties of grain—how they grow and the work it takes to bring them to the

Daisy Mae's 90-year-old hands still skillfully knead bread dough.

table. This walnut cake is delicious and special to us because we have walnut trees *and* plum trees here at the farm. The work for the cake starts with all of us sitting around the table cracking walnuts, anticipating the plums that have become precious dried sweet reminders of summer.

1 cup pitted dried Italian plums (prunes)
3 tablespoons cognac, divided
¾ cup sifted all-purpose flour
½ teaspoon kosher salt
¾ teaspoon baking powder
8 tablespoons (1 stick) unsalted butter, room temperature
1½ cups organic sugar (evaporated cane juice)
5 eggs
½ cup finely ground walnuts (a flourlike consistency)
1 cup chopped walnuts

Soak the Italian plums in 2 tablespoons of the cognac for at least 30 minutes (add a little water if they are really dry). Meanwhile, preheat the oven to 350 degrees F. Butter and lightly flour a 9-inch round cake pan. Remove plums with a slotted spoon, finely chop, and reserve. Sift, then measure the flour, and then sift together with the salt and baking powder.

Beat the butter in a stand mixer for 1 minute, then add the sugar and beat for 3 to 5 minutes until fluffy. Add the eggs, one at a time, scraping the sides of the bowl several times. Mix in the ground walnuts. Sift the dry ingredients over the batter, mixing just until combined. Fold in the remaining tablespoon of the cognac, the chopped walnuts, and the reserved plums.

Spread the batter into the prepared cake pan and bake 50 minutes to 1 hour, or until the cake is dark brown and a knife inserted comes out clean. Allow to cool in the pan for 10 to 15 minutes before unmolding. Store at room temperature for up to 2 days or freeze for up to 1 month.

WINTER PANTRY

Spelt Granola

MAKES 8 SERVINGS

Here is another great use for spelt. Serve this granola with milk, Quark, or plain yogurt. Top with poached dried fruits in winter and fresh fruit in summer, or simply eat it by the handful.

1 cup (2 sticks) unsalted butter

½ cup brown sugar

¾ cup snowberry honey or clover honey

1 teaspoon kosher salt

½ teaspoon vanilla

½ teaspoon freshly grated nutmeg

2 pounds rolled spelt

Preheat the oven to 350 degrees F.

In a small saucepan, melt the butter over medium heat. Add the brown sugar, honey, salt, vanilla, and nutmeg. Stir over medium heat until the sugar is dissolved.

Put the rolled spelt in a large mixing bowl. Pour the butter mixture over the spelt and toss until thoroughly coated. Spread the mixture on a large baking sheet and bake for about 12 to 15 minutes, stirring and turning occasionally until lightly browned.

Let the mixture cool on the baking sheet. Break up any clumps into smaller bits. Store in an airtight container in the pantry for up to 1 month.

Lamb–Potato Sausage

MAKES 10 POUNDS

This sausage is an ode to my Scandinavian roots: warm spice notes of coriander and nutmeg and the thrifty use of potatoes to help make the meat go farther. A little fennel is thrown in for the days that I wish I were Italian. The sausage will turn a shade of purple from the oxidation of the potatoes.

3 pounds lamb meat, trimmed and cubed

2 pounds pork shoulder, trimmed and cubed

1 medium yellow onion, peeled and grated

2 tablespoons kosher salt

2 tablespoons ground coriander

2 tablespoons ground fennel seed

1 tablespoon freshly grated nutmeg

15 large waxy potatoes (about 5 pounds), peeled and grated

1 tablespoon olive oil

In a meat grinder, grind together the lamb and pork using a ⅜-inch die. Refrigerate the meat for 1 hour in an airtight container. Combine the meat, onion, salt, coriander, fennel seed, and nutmeg in a large mixing bowl.

In another bowl, cover the potatoes with ice water. After a few minutes, drain and squeeze them in a dish towel until dry. Add the potatoes to the meat mixture and combine thoroughly. Heat the oil in a small frying pan until it slides easily across the pan. Form a small test patty and fry. Taste the patty and correct the seasonings if needed. Make patties with remaining mixture and fry.

Note: The uncooked sausage may be frozen in bulk or patty form. It may also be stuffed into lamb casings and frozen if desired.

Having a pantry well stocked with home preserves is the key to eating local during winter.

Quillisascut Five-Spice Country Duck Pâté
MAKES 15 SERVINGS (1½-QUART TERRINE MOLD)

Serve this terrine with mustard, pickles, or poached fruit. The skins from the duck breasts can be rendered to make duck fat, which is delicious and useful for duck confit and cassoulet (see "Fall Recipes") as well as in potato hash and many other dishes.

4 egg yolks

½ cup heavy cream

½ loaf stale white bread, crust removed and cubed

1 tablespoon olive oil

1 small carrot, peeled and finely chopped

2 pounds pork shoulder, ground finely

2 tablespoons kosher salt

1 handful parsley, finely chopped

2 teaspoons Chinese five-spice powder

3 skinless duck breasts, lightly salted

2 tablespoons tawny port

Preheat the oven to 325 degrees F.

Honeyed Spelt Granola and yogurt are a quick breakfast for a chilly morning.

In a mixing bowl, beat the egg yolks with the heavy cream. Stir in the bread cubes to make a panada. Meanwhile, heat the olive oil in a small sauté pan and cook the carrots for a few minutes until soft. Remove from heat and reserve.

In a stand mixer, beat the ground pork with the salt until it has a batterlike consistency. Combine the panada, pork, and reserved carrots. Add the parsley and five-spice powder to the pork mixture.

In another sauté pan, sear the duck breasts until each side is just brown. Deglaze the pan with the port (note that the duck will not be cooked through at this point).

Lay half of the pork mixture in a terrine mold (line with plastic wrap for quick unmolding). Lay the duck breasts, end to end, down the center of the mold. Carefully lay the remaining pork mixture around and on top of the duck breasts, smoothing to remove any air bubbles.

Cover the mold and place it inside a deep, ovenproof baking dish. Fill the baking dish with hot water about three-quarters of the way up the side of the mold. Cook in the oven in the water bath until the internal temperature is 158 degrees F. Cool in a water bath until the mold is ready to handle.

Unmold the terrine and refrigerate until thoroughly chilled. Slice and serve. This dish can be refrigerated for up to 2 weeks or frozen for up to 3 months.

Cajeta Sauce

MAKES 4 CUPS

Cajeta is a goat's milk caramel sauce that is wonderful on just about anything. At Quillisascut Farm we eat it by the spoonful, pour it over cinnamon rolls, ice cream, and bread pudding—we even spread it on toast. The goat's milk adds a characteristic tang to the caramel; there is no substitute for goat's milk, as it wouldn't be "cajeta" without it. Goat's milk is readily available in most supermarkets and co-op markets.

1 gallon goat's milk
3 cups organic sugar (evaporated cane juice)
1 cassia stick or cinnamon stick
1 teaspoon baking soda

In a large saucepot, bring the goat's milk, sugar, and cassia stick to a rapid simmer. Watch the pot carefully in the beginning to ensure it doesn't boil over. Continue simmering to reduce the liquid by half.

In a separate small saucepan, over medium heat, combine 1 cup of the hot liquid with the baking soda, stirring briskly. The mixture will foam and begin to caramelize. Continue stirring until the mixture is thickened and has turned a nice caramel brown.

Return this caramel to the larger saucepot and stir (the mixture may foam again initially). Continue cooking until the liquid is thick and caramel colored. When the mixture coats the back of a spoon, you have a sauce. Continue cooking a few more minutes and you'll get a thicker, jamlike consistency. Check for desired consistency by pouring a little on a plate and putting it into the refrigerator until cool. Remove and discard the cassia stick. Cajeta may be served warm or cold. Store refrigerated in sterilized jars for up to 1 month.

Variations: Substitute cardamom, star anise, or a dried chile for the cassia stick.

SPRING
RENEWAL

SPRING
RENEWAL

SPRING COMES LATE to the hills of eastern Washington. The last frost date most years is around May 10, but before that there are often thaws, where first flowers will poke through frozen ground and bloom. The next week a snowstorm will have the place looking like January again. Nonetheless, there's a feeling that winter's truly over, that the earth is stirring. The Huckleberry Mountain range rises to the east, patches of snow still clinging to the hills here and there. The crisp, cold air is a cacophony of messages—the twitter and chirp of starlings, crows, and black-capped chickadees; the hoots of wild turkeys calling back and forth across the fields; the dog's bark echoing off the hills; the rooster's awkward crowing leading it all. The pines are silent, as if waiting for the inevitable wind that rises up midmorning. And as the sun rises and the fields are illuminated in cool shadows and light, you can see that winter's browns and greys and whites have given way to every shade of new green you can imagine.

THE FARM AT DAWN:
MILKING THE GOATS

Six AM and already the cold April sun is edging through the curtains and across the wooden floor of the Quillisascut Farm bunkhouse. Lora Lea and Rick have pulled on their boots and ambled out of their house, nestled between the barn and gardens, down to the milking shed. Visitors at the farm are up, too—wanting to live, if even for a few days, like farmers.

The Misterlys' barn is no Martha Stewart affair. Painted dark brown and weather-worn, it is a working barn, especially at six AM. This part of the morning, more than any other, is a process, a system, that after twenty years seems to run itself. The goats line up as if they were in some goaty army, knowing exactly who goes first through the little door from the corral into the milking shed. They come in sets of five, and a list posted on the milking shed wall to remind Rick of the order in which to let them in reads like a Who's Who of movie stars and debutantes—Zelda, Petunia, Pamalot. One by one, the

Hand milking keeps the Misterlys in touch with herd health and establishes the daily rhythm of the farm.

goats walk up a wooden ramp onto the little waist-high balcony that has metal gates to keep them in place and buckets full of grain to occupy them.

Each goat has its place in the lineup—a short-bodied goat must go in the middle of the five, a rangy one at each end. Some are kickers and have to have one rear hoof tied back to a post. But milking is a relief for the goats, especially in spring after their kids are weaned. Once the kids stop drinking from their mothers, milking happens only twice a day, at six AM and four PM—not often enough for these lactation machines. If they keep getting milked, the mothers continue to produce as much as their bodies can handle, so

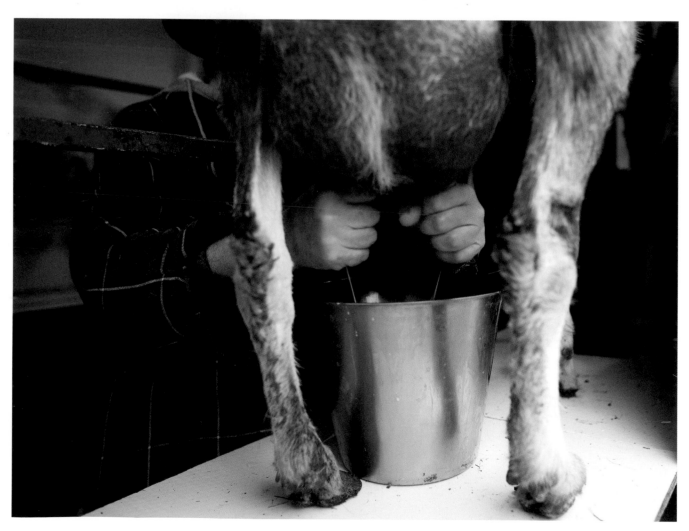

Rick gets a kiss while checking on goat mothers and their young kids.

they end up uncomfortable twice a day, waiting for relief. But unlike industrial dairy cows that are given hormones to continue and increase milk production, these goats almost stop giving milk altogether for a few months each year—a refreshing break for both goat and milker. Because they eat grass and whatever else they can find in the fields, the goats produce milk that changes taste throughout the year, in a consistent seasonal cycle. When they "freshen," or begin to provide milk for their kids, the milk is fresh and grassy, as is the fresh chèvre made from it. As the year goes on and the freshest grass is gone, the milk and the cheese become more "goaty" and intensely flavored.

Rick gets started with the first group of five (there are eight groups, about forty goats in all), with the *whish whish* of the brush as he and Lora Lea—and whoever else is helping—brush down the stiff brown and white hair around the teats to remove dirt. Then Rick pulls each teat, sending a little spray of milk into a bucket and pouring it into a dish for the waiting family of barn cats. This step makes for a clean milking (and clean milk).

Now the real milking begins. Lora Lea's hands are square and strong, pulling milk from each teat with a loud *ting* into the bucket. For most of the year—the nine months when the goats are milked—the Misterlys do this job, twice a day with no days off, by themselves. But since the farm school started in 2002, and especially over the past few years with the addition of an eager culinary student intern or two who want to learn the life of the farm, spring milking involves three or four sets of hands. In July and August the chefs, food lovers, home cooks, writers, and other students who visit the farm are eagerly up at six, ready to learn.

Not that the goats are happy about that. They like routine. They like the same knowledgeable hands that can get the job done fast, just as everything on the farm likes routine. Farming is all about collaboration—between the seed and the sun, the farmer and the friend. There is no abundance here without love between people and things. Each morning, the farm cats wait for the first streams of milk to be passed their way. And when the milking is done, the chickens, ducks, and guinea hens know their turn for grain and new water is coming.

On this morning Rick, Lora Lea, and an intern, Jackie Freeman, are moving the girls through the line as quickly as they can. Lora Lea stops to give a milking lesson when she needs to. "Make sure you squeeze from the top of the teat," she says. "Don't let the milk squirt back up into the udder." She deftly wraps her hand around the nipple from the top down and a strong stream hisses into the stainless-steel bucket. If this wrong-way milking happens, which it often does when you're learning, you can feel it, and the goat doesn't like it. "It can hurt the goat, create infection," Lora Lea says. After a morning of milking, something as simple as picking up a coffee cup makes you aware of the small muscles in your hands and of how the ease of city living can keep us from knowing that kind of basic but intricate physical work.

Rick pokes his head out of the milking barn and yells for the next bunch. "Blondie, Lainis, Pearl, Crumpet!" Or "Come on, get up, Zelda! Over here! No, Natalie's first, then you!" He's calling the goats like old ladies to a sewing bee, and they come—some are reluctant, others are waiting by his side. One by one, they move through the doorway into the shed, bleary-eyed. But each morning, just as the sun rises, this gathering, this process brings the community together—the goats and their tenders—to the work at hand.

STARTING THE GARDEN

After milking, everyone goes back to the house to brew a strong pot of French-press coffee. Jackie makes some spelt-meal pancakes with apple butter and plum jam preserved from last summer's harvest, and they talk about the day. Jackie tells what she, Lora Lea, and Kären have accomplished in the first few weeks she's been at the farm. "I've never planted *anything* before this," she says. "I have one houseplant that's a jade tree, and my brother waters that!" She laughs and stops to think. "It is so fun to cook here. You go out and get duck eggs and make pasta from them. You go to the garden to find what's out there." She speaks with the voice of many of the chefs who will come to the farm this summer. The young ones are mostly city kids whose passion and curiosity have driven them to want to know more about the wonders of food, to travel to its source, and to find something of themselves in the process as well.

Jackie heads back outside to the greenhouse—again, fairly makeshift, not English-conservatory style—and points to the rows of small plants waiting there until the ground is warm enough in the garden to nurture the tender roots. There must be ten varieties of peppers, with lovely or intriguing names like Ancho Gigantea and Chervena Chushka. These are all "heirloom" pepper varieties—that is, the seeds they are grown from have been saved and passed down from gardener to gardener.

The beds for the freshly planted tomato plants are lined with straw mulch that suppresses weeds, protects underlying soil, and holds in moisture.

Chef Kären Jurgensen tests a cattail shoot while foraging in a tributary of Quillisascut Creek.

The rows and rows of plants are all tagged. The number of different types of plants at the farm is amazing, but it's not surprising. Biodiversity is an important topic of discussion at Quillisascut. The term has been around for some time. In 1992 the United Nations Earth Summit in Rio de Janeiro defined biodiversity as "the variability among living organisms from all sources, including, among other things, terrestrial, marine, and other aquatic ecosystems, and the eco-logical complexes of which they are part: this includes diversity within species, between species, and of ecosystems." This definition was also adopted by the United Nations Convention on Biological Diversity.

In their daily menus and in the classes they will teach this summer, Lora Lea and Kären encourage honoring the different varietal names of plants or breeds of livestock as a way of introducing these items to their guests and celebrating the variety and bounty that have come down from farmers and gardeners throughout history. From beans (Lazy Housewife) to tomatoes (Mortgage Lifter) to poultry (French Marans), each plant and animal has a history that adds to the pleasure of growing, preparing, and eating it. "These are gifts of inheritance; they definitely bring beauty into our lives," says Lora Lea. But more than this, she believes biodiversity is important in another way: the genetic bounty of growing a large variety of foods on the farms is important in unlocking good health, improving nutrition, and fighting disease.

Summer farm interns prepare the soil for planting.

PLANTING BY THE LIGHT OF THE MOON

Getting the garden ready for plants and seeds is an important spring ritual—and a big job. This year, some high school students from West Sound Academy in Poulsbo, Washington, came out to the farm with their instructor, Judith Weinstock, to help mulch the garden as a community-service project. They turned the compost pile—created over the year by layering garden clippings, kitchen scraps, dried leaves, and

Apricot blossoms tell us it is time to plant potatoes and peas, as Rick rototills the garden.

straw until it cooks into a dark, nutrient-rich "black gold"—with shovels, adding more old straw into the compost. Then they mulched the garden plots by hand, spreading the warm, dark compost along the beds and turning it into the garden soil, helping to loosen the farm's top layer of dense clay. Finally, the high school students laid down a layer of fresh straw between the beds, creating pathways to help people avoid walking on the young plants.

Lora Lea and Jackie have done their early March and April plantings by following the *Kimberton Hills Biodynamic Agriculture Planting Guide & Calendar*—sort of a more intense *Old Farmer's Almanac*. The squares on the calendar suggest a schedule that might draw order to the chaos that nature can seem to be: February 25, plant roots, it says. Waxing gibbous moon: start onions and leeks. Lora Lea has written in an exultant hand next to that day's entry: "Fresh Snow!"

Although Quillisascut is not a completely biodynamic farm, the Misterlys appreciate and abide by some of the tenets of biodynamics. This philosophy was first established by the Austrian scientist and philosopher Rudolf Steiner in a series of eight lectures in Germany in 1924. Farmers across Europe have observed its tenets for decades, and most recently the philosophy is finding a following in the wine industry in France and throughout Europe, as well as increasingly in the United States, especially in California. The basic idea is that the optimum quality in any agricultural product can be obtained if the cycles of the moon and the sun are considered. So the best time for pruning is when the moon is new and the yearly cycle is at a low ebb, while the plant's (and the soil's) energy is lessened. Conversely, the best time for harvesting is when the moon is full and the earth's "outward" energy is at its peak.

AN IN-BETWEEN SEASON

Midmorning, after feeding the chickens and guinea hens, and moving the ducks' mobile pen to a new spot where they can peck at grass and their waste can fertilize a new set of grapevines, we are back in the kitchen. "Everything is doing something out there," Lora Lea says. It is truly a time of renewal. "In springtime, you are working, but there is a balance between doing and planning. In summertime, you are just doing. Spring is an even time of year, when you feel things aren't out of control yet."

Some birds have been here all winter—LBJs ("little brown jobs," as birders call them). As spring approaches, more and more birds come onto the scene, and the farm becomes theater: the bright costumes of house finches with red breasts blend into brown bodies; flamboyant orange-breasted orioles swoop and glide; robins return with a crescendo of sound, making a raucous ruckus in the bushes at four AM. When they first arrive early in spring, the robins eat what is left of winter berries and stay away from new plants and feeders, but after a day or two they are totally bold, diving after whatever fresh

nourishment they can find. And when the late-afternoon sun comes out, the hummingbirds flock to the feeders in what can only be called troop formation, taking turns, intent on the sugar-water feast that Lora Lea's mother has set up for them.

Yesterday a downy woodpecker hopped around the base of the tree. With his black-striped face, black wings with white spots, and white belly, he kept to his business. This is springtime: every plant, every animal, bird, and bug is focused on the business at hand—growing, pushing forward, finding the new path toward the ultimate purpose of life—nourishment and growth.

THE CHALLENGES OF FARM TIME

As we sit for a short break between chores, Lora Lea tells us about the early days of the farm, the uncertainty, the community that has taken years to build. "When we first moved here, our neighbors would say, 'You can't grow that here.' What they really meant was that you wouldn't risk growing that here. Seed is valuable. If you aren't sure of a crop, why take the risk? Those neighbors came from a generation that wasn't willing to risk anything, because you had to live off what you grew. It was an Old World way of thinking—'What will carry us through?'"

Things are not so different now, though. Few would go out and buy a new tree—an almond tree, for instance—just to see if it grew. "Every year we are making decisions about what to plant," Lora Lea says. "How much time do you have to deal with milking, fencing, weeding?" For a moment she looks as if she has the weight of the year, the full year's work of the farm, on her mind. Time slows, in winter, but when things gear up and the garden takes off, there is so much work you don't have time to think. "Do you have time to plant more raspberries?" she says. "And then, what will you do with them?"

The opportunities seem to be endless, if not overwhelming. Lora Lea's friends and neighbors John and Janet Crandall (see the farm profile of Riverview Orchard in the "Fall Preservation"

Farm Profile: Mingo Mountain Apiary
Stephan Schott, Beekeeper, Rice, Washington

Beekeeper Stephan Schott of Mingo Mountain Apiary, just a few miles from Quillisascut Farm, comes to the school each summer to give apiary demonstrations and to visit some of his bees that live in a beebox at Quillisascut from spring to fall, doing their work of pollinating crops and other plants. Schott is passionate about these fascinating creatures. First he gives a "bee primer" about the habits of bees—the roles of the queen, the female workers (who gather nectar and pollen and transfer pollen from plant to plant), and the male drones. The one purpose of the drones is to mate with the queen when she performs her nuptial flight; she may mate with more than one drone, an act that is fatal to the drone.

"Honey is an edible record of what happened in the summer," Schott says. "It sums up summer and connects us to that fruitful time." He offers several different types of honey for students to taste—snowberry (a Northwest native in the honeysuckle family, and his pride and joy), fireweed, and clover—the nectar drawn primarily from these sources, then "miraculously transformed" into the golden honey. After the tasting, Schott dons his white beekeeper's suit and netted headgear and takes the students to the beebox, just a few dozen yards from the bunkhouse. He lights a bit of dried grass in his small smoker and pumps it into the hive to calm the bees, then takes the lid off the box. "I may visit a hundred hives in a day," he says, "but every time I open one up, I find some new variation on the theme of tens of thousands of bugs living in harmony and collaborating for the success of their colony."

Schott had his "first look inside a beehive" in 1973, when an elderly neighbor offered a share of the honey if he'd help harvest it. "I was immediately entranced and captivated by this mysterious, bustling enterprise," he says, and he's been involved with honeybees ever since, tending hives all over the Northwest and down into California. Collaboration and cooperation, he believes, are essential lessons we can learn from observing bees: "There is no better example of an ideally cooperative society than a hive of honeybees."

Pulling out one of the racks, with its intricate construction of hexagonal wax cells full of honey, Schott lets students look closely and even taste the bees' harvest. "Honey is a truly local food," he says. And indeed, it is sweet and a bit earthy, with a rich flavor that blossoms in your mouth; you can imagine the bees visiting the same plants on these hills over and over and returning, full of nectar and covered with pollen, to the hive.

Schott talks about honey's healing properties, and its complex collection of enzymes that help boost the human immune system—not to mention the carbohydrates that give us energy. "Sadly, honey has been overlooked in the kitchen and on the table in this age of granulated sugar," he says. He feels keeping bees benefits both the environment and his local farmland, and he hopes his work with these fascinating creatures will help "renew and strengthen the partnership between cooks and honey."

chapter) have taken on this challenge with their orchards and raspberry patches. Just like Rick and Lora Lea, the Crandalls fit their side business—roasting and shipping coffee—in among their farm chores, such as pruning trees, picking fruit, preparing it, boxing it, and shipping it—all on a seasonal cycle according to what is happening on the farm.

Although the daily routine of the farm goes on throughout the year, once the days start to get longer and warmer and the garden starts to grow, life speeds up. This is true on any farm, but Quillisascut has many functions: not only does the farm provide food for its owners, it's also a goat cheese busi-

Mushrooms, like the giant *Boletus*, add a mysterious complexity to the earth's bounty in spring.

ness and a school. Here, spring is a time of renewed energy and ramping up for the busy summer to come. Lora Lea's diary entries capture this urgency.

April 16: *The hum is back, the list grows: Prepare the soil for planting and smooth out the beds; pot up the tomato, eggplant, and pepper plants started in flats in the greenhouse; transplant out the lettuce, cabbage, and onions; get the schedule made out for the students that will be arriving next weekend; make the beds. Oh, this is starting to sound repetitive with lots of different summer guests needing their beds made—from friends, family, and students, to the garden guests that are ready to arrive, potatoes, peas, fava beans, carrots, and onward through the summer's bounty. Here we go!*

Opposite: In spring the goats are anxious to get out on the lush green pasture.

Above: Rick explains to students that goat manure from the barn is one of the most valuable products the farm produces.

April 20: *Here on the farm we are still sitting on the edge of spring (yesterday it snowed on the brilliant daffodils). The goats are finished kidding except for two stragglers. Thoughts of summer meals are growing in flats in front of the big windows in the form of onion sprouts. Today when I lifted the clear plastic covers, the plants were all poking out of the ground. Onions come up bent in half, touching their toes, and some of them were even ready to unfold and stand up straight, saluting the sun.*

The heirloom tomatoes, peppers, and eggplant are ready to transplant from the seed trays to pots. Cabbage and lettuce would love to get set out in the garden, yet on a morning like today,

Chef Profile: Emily Crawford
Boulette's Larder, San Francisco, California

At Boulette's Larder, a shop and restaurant in San Francisco's Ferry Terminal, the chefs source all their ingredients locally with principles that are respectful of taste, the environment, and social justice. The shop is a larder for the home cook, supplying the basics, including stocks, rendered fats, condiments, prepared vegetables, grains, and meat. But Boulette's is also a restaurant that serves breakfast and lunch in a small dining room, with one communal table literally in the kitchen. In the evenings it hosts private dinners for groups of up to twenty-four people, with a set menu.

Emily Crawford was attracted to Boulette's unique concept, and the experiences she had at Quillisascut prepared her for her work with fresh ingredients at the restaurant. "The food traditions we are preserving by continuing to practice them are important in the future of food. Sourcing our ingredients from local farmers and artisans is also an incredibly important aspect of my job." Crawford is proud to be affiliated with the strong commitment Amaryll Schwertner and Lori Regis of Boulette's

have established to supporting exceptional local products. This makes her job part of the ongoing evolution toward a better appreciation for where our food comes from and how it is produced.

"Spending a week with Rick and Lora Lee at their farm was an integral part of my current line of thought on cooking and food," she says. "Sharing a meal with people creates an arena for discussion and collaboration that may not work its way into many other parts of our day. I became profoundly aware of the importance of this while at Quillisascut. Having each meal prepared with ingredients from the farm or neighboring farms, and by the hands of one of us, created a deep connection to the food we were eating." Crawford says she realized that her career could and would affect people and create change. By being an advocate and supporter of more sustainable food systems, she subtly helps people become more aware of and concerned with what they are eating.

with frost everywhere and ice three-eighths of an inch thick on the water buckets, we wait on spring warmth to push the last frost out of the earth.

The tangy aromas of cultured milk once again waft from the cheese room, and wheels of cheese are lining the aging-room shelves. It always seems to me that the spring and fall equinoxes are a time for centering, feeling whole, and filling, everything comes together for this brief section of time—and then off and running toward the future, scattered!

The end of May and the first of June are what Lora Lea calls her "panic dates" for planting. "We are sitting on the edge of spring and planning for the abundance of summer," she says. "Get it in now, or forget about it." She laughs, but it's true. The ground has begun to warm (it must be frost-free before tender roots can grow). All of the garden starts that are in the greenhouse are either planted (tomatoes) or sitting out getting acclimated to the weather (peppers and eggplant).

Lora Lea teaches culinary arts students how to make mozzarella cheese from the product of that morning's milking.

Chef Profile: Christine Keff
Flying Fish, Seattle, Washington

When you are out to dinner and you ask the average restaurant server or chef where the lettuce in your salad came from, you might get a blank stare. But not so at Flying Fish restaurant in Seattle. Chef Christine Keff wanted to make a statement of support for local agriculture, so in 2004 she contracted with Mike and Shelley Verdi of Whistling Train Farm, just south of Seattle, to grow the produce for Flying Fish's all-organic menu. Keff's action voiced a strong commitment to using local seasonal ingredients. When the chef spends less time on sourcing local produce and the farmer spends less time on marketing, both are liberated to get on with the business of cooking fresh, vibrant meals or growing a vital, healthy crop.

"Our relationship is still forming, even after a few years," says Keff. "It's been a learning experience for all of us. Mike and Shelley have had to figure out our needs and how to plan for them. We in the kitchen have had to rethink the way we plan for the menu. In a global economy, we are so used to being able to pick up the phone and get whatever we want whenever we want it. Now we live with the realities of Mother Nature. The relationship has been and continues to be rewarding and enlightening, pushing us all to grow. So it will be fun to see where we end up."

May 20: *We have been hustling to plant all the beans—those that like to climb and twist around a pole and the bush types that hover close to the ground. The maroon and white–speckled Jacob's Cattle beans are in, along with the Italian White cannellini and French flageolet (along with the ducklings, they have us shouting, "Cassoulet!"). We have planted a row of Provider bush green beans with the goal of fancy pickled dilly beans on my mind.*

The cucumbers are starting to come up in the main garden. Northern Pickling is our main crop, along with Parisian Pickling and True Lemon cukes. Down by the school and in the greenhouse we have planted some of the smooth-skin "burpless" types for slicing with summer meals.

It is the mad dash to get it all planted and maintained, then finding places to stick in, here and there, that "one more" item. A garden is like a patchwork quilt of color and texture, where all the pieces fit together to cover our needs, from nurturing the soil to filling our bellies.

It is hot these last days of May and too hot to put out those last transplants—rain and cool weather are better for setting out the tender plants. We are waiting for the rainy weather that is forecast. Then in will go those melons, peppers, and eggplant, and the garden will be on its way.

Peppers are subtropical plants, so they are among the last to be transplanted from the greenhouse. Fish peppers are RAFT listed.

Chickens: Biodiversity and the Feathered Flock

There is a myth that eggs with brown or tan shells are better for you or have less cholesterol than white-shelled eggs. In truth, eggs from different breeds are very similar. The feed that the birds eat has a greater effect on the flavor and health benefits of their eggs than does their breed. Chickens that are raised in pastures or are fed greens have darker, almost orange yolks high in Vitamin E; their eggs have a more robust flavor. Although most of the chickens used for meat at the farm are purchased from Paul's Pastured Poultry, Lora Lea and Rick do keep some chickens for eggs—and also just because they love chickens. Here are some of the breeds that live on Quillisascut Farm:

The *Araucana* breed was brought to the United States from South America in the 1920s. They are gaining popularity for their natural blue-green eggshells, which look beautiful nestled alongside the brown Marans eggs. The Araucana is a dual-purpose bird, used for both egg production and meat. A slightly curved beak, ear tufts, and rounded tail feathers that earn them the description "rumpless" set these birds apart from the Ameraucana. *Ameraucanas* lay blue- and green-colored eggs and have earmuffs—a pair of feathery fluffs below their ears that look like plump chipmunk cheeks—and upright tail feathers.

Cornish Cross chickens, a cross between the White Cornish and the White Plymouth Rock, are the classic white bird with a red crest and yellow feet. These fast-growing birds are bred primarily for meat; their main activities are eating or sitting by the feed trough waiting for food.

Marans is a dual-purpose breed from France, known for its beautiful chocolate-brown eggs. They are strong, healthy birds that do well wandering a pasture, eating insects and vegetation. They have black-and-white feathering similar to that of the Barred Rock.

Turkens, with their featherless necks, definitely stand out. Despite their name, they are 100 percent chicken. People sometimes mistake them for young turkeys or ask, "What happened to that bird?" With a spiffy feathered cap under a bright red comb and a neck naked down to the shoulder, these birds are unique. Their feather coloration includes white, buff, black, and red. They are good farmstead chickens, will hatch out their own chicks, and are great for both meat and eggs.

White Leghorns have bright white feathers and a large jaunty red comb that flops to one side. These birds are all business: they are prolific layers of white eggs and are the breed used in most large egg-producing operations.

Wyandottes have pale feathers edged in black, giving these birds a lacy look. This American breed is named after the Native American Wyandotte tribe of the Iroquois Nation. There are several variations in feather color—white with black, golden brown with black—yet all of the birds produce light tan eggs.

Libby the livestock guardian dog watches over Bardley the Bard Rock rooster.

SPRING
RECIPES

SPRINGTIME FLAVORS IN THE KITCHEN revolve around eggs, baby vegetables, and fresh herbs. Fresh soft cheeses like ricotta, fromage blanc, and chèvre are at their best this time of year, extra rich from the new mothers' milk. At Quillisascut we are still supplementing our diets with stored and cured items from fall, like bacon, ham, corn flours, and honey. A few wild foods around the farm are blossoming, and tasty morels are popping up in the mountains. These wild foods are precious little bonuses to our larder.

BREAKFAST & BREADS

Baby Beet Hash, Pork Belly, and Poached Eggs
MAKES 4 SERVINGS

A poached egg perched on top of colorful hash puts us in a good mood to start our spring work for the day. Use very fresh farm eggs for poaching; the whites will not spread too much, and the yolk will set up firm and high. Cook the pork belly and roast the beets the night before for easy assembly in the morning.

1 pound pork belly

2 cups apple cider

1 dried bay leaf

6 sprigs fresh thyme

5 whole black peppercorns

2 dried arbol or other chiles

12 baby beets, tops trimmed to ½ inch

Kosher salt

2 tablespoons bacon fat or olive oil

1 small yellow onion, diced

2 cloves garlic, minced

Coarsely ground black pepper

2 tablespoons chopped fresh chives

4 eggs

To prepare the pork belly, preheat the oven to 300 degrees F.

Put the pork belly in a small braising pot along with apple cider, bay leaf, thyme, black peppercorns, and chiles. Cover, place in the oven, and cook until fork-tender, about 2½ hours. Remove from the oven and cool in the braising liquid, until able to handle. Cut the pork belly in ⅜-inch-thick slices. Refrigerate in an airtight container until ready to use.

To roast the beets, preheat the oven to 400 degrees F.

Put the beets in a shallow baking dish or ovenproof skillet. Cover with water about halfway up the level of the beets. Sprinkle with kosher salt and place in the oven. Roast until fork-tender, about 20 minutes. Remove beets from the oven, cool in the pan, then peel and quarter.

In a large, heavy-bottomed skillet, melt the bacon fat or olive oil over medium heat. Stir in the onion and garlic, cooking until just translucent. Add the pork and beets, increase the heat to medium-high, and cook, turning occasionally as the hash begins to caramelize. Scrape from the bottom of the pan. Season with salt and pepper to taste. Toss in the chives. Set cover askew and keep warm until ready to serve.

Meanwhile, pour enough water into a shallow pan so that it will cover the eggs when you add them. Cover the pan and bring water to a boil. Carefully crack the eggs into the water, turn off the heat, and cover. The eggs are done when the whites are just set, about 3 minutes.

To assemble the dish, divide the hash among four bowls and top each with a poached egg.

Variations: Any leftover cooked meat can be substituted for the pork belly. Potatoes are also a welcome addition.

As the days warm up and daylight lengthens in spring, the chickens ramp up their production of eggs. Here they are featured in Baby Beet Hash, Pork Belly, and Poached Eggs.

Mandan Bride Corn Flour and Chive Scones

MAKES 8 SERVINGS

Mandan Bride corn is RAFT listed (See "Fall Preservation" chapter). Although this colorful corn flour makes these scones special, any corn flour can be substituted. After the fall corn harvest at Quillisascut, we hang flour corn ears to air-dry for storage, then simply remove the kernels and grind for fresh-milled cornmeal throughout the remaining seasons. We use local snowberry honey in this recipe, but any honey will do. Honey produced by your local beekeeper purportedly helps to prevent hay fever from local pollens. We like the snowberry honey because its flavor reflects our bioregion.

A basket full of shallots, cipollini, and red storage onions for Five Lilies Soup

2 cups bread flour

2 cups Mandan Bride corn flour

½ tablespoon kosher salt

2 tablespoons baking powder

¾ cup (1½ sticks) cold unsalted butter, cut into pieces

3 eggs

1¼ cups whole milk

¼ cup snowberry honey

2 tablespoons chopped fresh chives

Preheat the oven to 350 degrees F. Grease a baking sheet.

Using a mixer with a paddle attachment, or by hand, mix the bread flour, corn flour, salt, and baking powder. Add the butter pieces until the texture is like coarse crumbs. Mix in the eggs, one at a time, then add the milk and honey until just incorporated. Stir in the chives.

Form the dough into an 8-inch circle, place on the prepared baking sheet, and refrigerate covered for 1 hour. (The dough can also be frozen for later use.)

Place on the center rack in the oven and bake for 20 to 25 minutes, until golden and puffed. The center should be set when pressed with fingers. Let rest at room temperature for 10 minutes, then cut into wedges and serve with honey and butter if desired.

Seasonal variations: This recipe is a great base for playing with seasonal ingredients. In summer add grated summer squash and sautéed onions for a savory scone. In fall substitute whole wheat flour for corn flour and use sautéed pears and rosemary. In winter toss in dried fruits and walnuts poached in brandy. Simply stir these ingredients into the dough at the end of processing.

SOUPS & SALADS

Five Lilies Soup
MAKES 8 SERVINGS

A delicate name for a soup honoring the often pungent, yet sweet when cooked, *Allium* genus. Consisting of hundreds of varieties, both wild and cultivated, commonly known as onions, garlic, leeks, scallions, ramps, and so on, lilies have been eaten since prehistoric times and are of great importance in the kitchen. They are the base of most stocks and sauces, the aromatics in the braise, and the underpinnings of a well-made soup. If you are in the mood to gild the lily, so to speak, top this soup off with a garnish of a pretty cheese-stuffed daylily.

4 tablespoons (½ stick) unsalted butter, divided

1½ cups finely diced sweet onion

1½ cups finely diced red onion

¾ cup finely diced shallots

2 dried bay leaves

8 to 10 whole black peppercorns

2 cups chopped leeks, both white and tender green part

2 cloves garlic, minced

½ cup white wine

4 cups chicken or vegetable stock

1 cup heavy cream

Freshly ground black pepper

Kosher salt

¼ clove nutmeg, freshly grated

1½ tablespoons chopped fresh chives

In a 2-quart stockpot, melt half of the butter over low heat. Add the sweet onion, red onion, shallots, bay leaves, and peppercorns. Cover and cook until the onions are translucent.

Uncover and increase heat to medium. Cook until the onion begins to caramelize, stirring occasionally. Add the remaining butter, leeks, garlic, and white wine. Cook for another 10 minutes, until the leeks are soft. Pour in the stock and simmer, covered, for 20 minutes.

Remove soup from stockpot and purée in batches in a food processor or with an immersion blender. Return puréed soup to the stockpot and add the heavy cream, black pepper, salt, and nutmeg. Simmer for 15 minutes more, uncovered, or until the soup is thickened slightly by the cream. Adjust salt seasonings if necessary. Stir in chives and serve hot.

Seasonal variations: In the winter months you can use storage onions and omit the leeks and chives for a "four-lilies" version.

Wild Rose Petal Vinaigrette
MAKES 2 CUPS

Wild roses abound along the edges of Quillisascut Farm. In spring we gather the fragrant petals, and in fall we search out the hips for making syrups. This light vinaigrette is nice with tender spring lettuces, leaves, and wild weeds. Unlike most vinaigrettes, it contains no pepper, which would overpower the delicate rose flavor. We toss rose petals into the salad for extra color. Dried rose petals, available at your local herbalist or natural-foods store, may be substituted; use about half the quantity, and steep them in water first. *Do not use rose petals from bushes that have been sprayed.* Rosewater is available at specialty markets.

1 shallot, minced

½ cup finely cut fresh rose petals

1 tablespoon chopped fresh Italian parsley

1 tablespoon chopped fresh basil

2 tablespoons rosewater

¾ cup light white wine vinegar

1 teaspoon mild-flavored local honey, such as wildflower, fireweed, or clover

Pinch of kosher salt

1½ cups organic canola oil

Put the shallots, rose petals, parsley, basil, rosewater, and white wine vinegar into a blender and let sit for 20 minutes. Add the honey and salt, then purée. Slowly drizzle in the canola oil and blend until emulsified. Adjust salt to taste.

English Pea Soup, Green Garlic Flan, and Pea-Shoot Salad
MAKES 4 SERVINGS

This pretty chilled green soup looks and tastes like spring. It can be made a day ahead. Green garlic is very young garlic, available only in the springtime, from your farmers market or produce department. When choosing green garlic, look for the soft-neck varieties; the hard-neck varieties will have a tough, hard core. Verjus, the juice from unripened grapes, is available bottled at specialty stores, some wineries, and many grocers.

Flan:

½ cup finely chopped green garlic

1 cup heavy cream

1 whole egg plus one yolk

⅛ teaspoon salt

Pinch of freshly ground black pepper

Dash of freshly grated nutmeg

Unsalted butter for ramekins

Soup:

2 shallots, finely diced

2 teaspoons unsalted butter

2 cups shelled English peas, blanched

A cool version of pea soup

2 tablespoons chopped fresh mint

½ cup heavy cream

1½ cups vegetable stock

Kosher salt

Splash of champagne vinegar or verjus

Garnish:

¼ cup fresh baby pea shoots, tossed with a splash of olive oil

For the flan:

Preheat the oven to 350 degrees F.

In heavy saucepan, put the garlic and heavy cream over low heat. Heat to scalding, when bubbles just begin to form on the edge of the pan. Remove from heat, and let steep for 10 minutes. Strain out and discard the garlic. Set the liquid aside until cool, then whisk in the eggs until frothy. Stir in the salt, pepper, and nutmeg.

Grease 4 small ramekins and divide custard among them. Put them in a shallow pan and pour in hot water until it comes about three-quarters of the way up the sides of the ramekins. Place in the center of the oven and bake until just set, about 15 minutes. Refrigerate until ready to serve.

For the soup:

In a small saucepan, sweat the shallots in butter over medium heat. Cool briefly in the pan. In a food processor, purée the shallots, English peas, mint, heavy cream, stock, salt, and champagne vinegar or verjus. Add more stock to reach the desired consistency. Strain. Adjust seasoning

For the assembly:

To remove the flans from their ramekins, dip the base of each in hot water, run a knife around the edge of each flan, and turn them out into 4 serving bowls. Don't worry if the top edges are a bit shaggy—they will be covered by the soup. Pour the soup around the flans, top each with pea shoots, and serve.

Variation: Roasted beets in place of peas would make a dramatic and beautiful soup.

ENTRÉES

Forager's Pappardelle with Fresh Favas,
Scapes, and Asparagus

MAKES 2 SERVINGS

A mid-May-to-early-June trip to the farmers market should provide you with the ingredients for this vegetarian pasta dish. If you have trouble sourcing the wild ingredients, simply omit the exotic mushrooms or substitute cultivated mushrooms; baby spinach would work well as a substitute for the wood violets. Fresh pasta can be handmade or purchased at a specialty market. When shopping for garlic scapes, look for bright green color to the very tips. The seed bud on the top should be small and firm, with no evidence of seeds. Stalks should be firm but not woody. Morels should be moist but not wet—and free of worms. Be sure

to tap out any sand (particularly sandy morels need to be soaked and patted dry before using). Fiddlehead ferns should be green and tightly coiled; avoid those with brown centers.

½ cup wood violets (leaves, tender stems, and flowers)

4 whole garlic scapes, trimmed 2 to 3 inches from the bottom of the stalk

10 ounces uncooked fresh pasta, pappardelle cut

2 tablespoons olive oil

2 tablespoons (¼ stick) unsalted butter

¼ pound fresh morel mushrooms, cleaned and trimmed

2 cloves garlic, thinly sliced

Kosher salt

1 tablespoon whole fennel seed

1 spring onion, julienned

6 stalks asparagus, peeled and sliced on the diagonal

¼ cup whole fiddlehead ferns (optional), cleaned and trimmed

¼ cup cider vinegar

¼ cup white wine

½ cup blanched, shelled, and peeled fava beans (from about 20 pods, depending on size)

Cracked black pepper

¼ cup fromage blanc, room temperature

High-quality extra-virgin olive oil for drizzling

Soak the wood violets in tepid water for 15 minutes, drain, and spin dry. Reserve.

In a pot of boiling salted water, blanch the garlic scapes for 2 minutes, remove from the water and reserve. Add the pasta and cook for about 3 minutes. Drain and toss with a little bit of the olive oil. Reserve.

Forager's Pappardelle with Fresh Favas, Scapes, and Asparagus

Melt the butter in a large sauté pan over medium heat. Add the morels and garlic, then season with salt. Remove mushrooms from the pan and reserve. Add the fennel seed and cook for 1 minute, then add the onion. Cook and stir until the onion caramelizes. Drizzle in the remaining olive oil and add the asparagus and fiddlehead ferns, cooking until bright green.

Pour in the cider vinegar and white wine and reduce the liquid by half. Decrease the heat and add the fava beans and reserved scapes and morels. Season with salt and pepper to taste. Mix in the cooked pasta, toss gently, and cook for about 2 minutes.

Divide the fromage blanc between two serving plates and top with the pasta and vegetables, distributing in a proportionate and appealing manner. Pour any remaining sauce over each plate. Top the pasta with the reserved wood violets, drizzle with extra virgin olive oil, and sprinkle with cracked black pepper.

Variations: Fresh peas could be substituted for fava beans in the spring. In early fall use chanterelles, roasted garlic, bulb fennel, and cherry tomatoes; top with fried sage leaves.

Nettle Gnocchi with Porcini, Spring Onions, and Egg
MAKES 4 SERVINGS

This is a simple Parisian-style gnocchi paired with the decadent porcini. The softly poached egg creates the sauce for a finishing touch. True spring onions are often sold as "salad onions" or "pink onions," but if you can't find either, red storage onions may be substituted. (But don't confuse spring onions with green onions or scallions! Spring onions are the first of the season.) Gnocchi can be made ahead in large batches and frozen on a sheet tray. After a day in the freezer, they can be put into bags and stored in the freezer for quick weeknight meals.

Gnocchi:

  2 tablespoons (¼ stick) unsalted butter

  1 cup water or milk

  1¼ cups all-purpose flour

  1 tablespoon kosher salt

  5 eggs

  1¼ cups (about 6 ounces) shredded semisoft cheese,
     such as Gouda

  ½ cup nettles, blanched and finely chopped
     (about 4 cups raw)

Assembly:

  4 eggs

  1 large fresh porcini mushroom, sliced ¼-inch thick

  6 tablespoons (¾ stick) unsalted butter, divided

  Salt and pepper

  2 spring onions, julienned

  2 cloves garlic, thinly sliced

  ½ cup fresh pea shoots

  Freshly grated Parmesan (optional)

For the gnocchi:

Heat the butter and water in a heavy-bottomed 2-quart sauce-pot. Stir in the flour and salt, and cook over medium heat until incorporated and the batter pulls away from the sides of the pot. Cook for about 3 minutes more, stirring constantly. Transfer the batter to a standing mixer bowl and add the eggs, one at a time, beating on high for at least 1 minute before adding another egg. The batter should be shiny but have some body. Mix in the cheese and nettles until incorporated.

Set a large pot of water to boil. Place the batter into a pastry bag without a tip and pipe the dough into boiling water, cutting or pinching off the dough every three-quarters of an inch. Gnocchi will float as they cook; allow them to float for about 2 minutes, or until soft yet firm. Gently skim them from the water, shake them free of water, and put them on an oiled baking sheet. Reserve.

For the poached eggs:

Pour enough water into a shallow pan to cover the eggs. Cover and bring to a boil. Carefully crack each egg into the water, turn off the heat, and cover. The eggs are done when the whites are just set, about 3 minutes.

For the assembly:

While the eggs are cooking, melt 3 tablespoons of the butter in a sauté pan over medium heat. Add the porcini and cook until brown, turning once. Season with salt and pepper to taste. Remove from pan and set aside. Add the onions and garlic to the pan, and cook until translucent. Stir in the remaining butter, melt, and toss in the gnocchi and reserved porcini. Cook for 1 minutes. Toss in the pea shoots.

Divide the gnocchi among 4 plates and top each with a poached egg. With a vegetable peeler, shave thin slices of Parmesan over the top and serve immediately.

Variations: If nettles are not available, any herb or even spinach may be substituted. A simple brown butter sauce served with the gnocchi would be delicious, as would pesto.

Chicken Stew with Ricotta–Chive Dumplings
MAKES 6 SERVINGS

Simple and light, this recipe makes use of leftover chicken. The turnips give a wonderful earthy flavor to the stew. Spring onions, sometimes sold as "salad onions," are the first onions of the year. Green garlic is in season in the spring; its flavor is milder and brighter than that of storage garlic. Using homemade stock is a core principle of the sustainable kitchen, and we strongly encourage it in our classes. Homemade stock has brighter flavors, less sodium, and more nutritional value than store-bought stock. It's also more economical and less wasteful.

Dumplings:

    2 cups (about 1 pound) ricotta cheese

    ½ cup chopped fresh chives

    1 egg

An alternative to traditional chicken and dumplings, this stew features dumplings of fresh ricotta cheese and utilizes the delicate produce of spring.

    1 cup cornmeal

    ½ cup all-purpose flour

    3 teaspoons kosher salt

Stew:

    2 tablespoons chicken fat or olive oil

    2 spring onions, chopped

    1 bunch (about 1 pound) baby carrots, cleaned
        and sliced on the diagonal

    1 bunch (about 8) baby turnips, trimmed and quartered

1 stalk green garlic (or 4 cloves regular garlic),
    thinly sliced

4 cups chicken stock

4 cups shredded roasted chicken

2 tablespoons chopped fresh thyme

Kosher salt

Freshly ground black pepper

For the dumplings:

In a medium bowl, mix together the ricotta, chives, egg, cornmeal, flour, and salt. Reserve.

For the stew:

In a large stockpot, melt the chicken fat over medium heat. Add the onions, carrots, turnips, and garlic, and cook until the onions are softened. Pour in the stock and reduce heat to simmer for about 15 minutes, until the vegetables are soft. Add the shredded chicken and thyme, and season to taste with salt and pepper. Cook 5 minutes more. The stew should be a bit brothy; if it's not, add a little water.

Drop the reserved dumplings into stew by the spoonful, cover and cook over medium-low heat for 7 minutes. Turn the dumplings over, cover, and cook for an additional 5 minutes. Serve hot.

Variations: For a fall or winter version of this dish, add potatoes and substitute sage for the chives in the dumplings. For a vegetarian version, omit the chicken; use water or vegetarian stock, and add kale, beet tops, and mustard greens.

Roast Quail with Elderflower Sauce
MAKES 2 SERVINGS

Elderflowers are plentiful in the spring; you will find them from your local forager and on hills and roadsides through-

out the Cascades and Rocky Mountains. If you can't locate elderflowers, substitute lavender flowers, sage flowers, or rosemary flowers in this recipe. Sautéed beet tops are an excellent accompaniment, providing a balance to the sweetness of the sauce. Another good pairing would be baby patty pans with lemon verbena (see Roasted Baby Pattypans with Lemon Verbena recipe later in this chapter).

1 cup organic sugar (evaporated cane juice)

1 cup water

2 cups chicken stock

2 bunches elderflowers on the stem

2 quail, trussed

1 tablespoon bacon fat or unsalted butter

1 teaspoon kosher salt

Preheat the oven to 400 degrees F.

In a small saucepan, combine the sugar and water, and bring to a simmer. Reduce syrup to 1 cup and reserve. In another saucepan, combine the chicken stock, reserved syrup, and elderflowers. Simmer gently, uncovered, until the liquid is reduced by half. Remove the elderflowers and strain the sauce. Return the sauce to the pan and continue to reduce until thick and syrupy. Reserve and keep warm.

Rub each quail liberally with bacon fat and salt (gently lift the skin from the breast and spread the fat and salt under the skin). Place the birds, breast side up, in a small roasting pan or skillet. Heat on stovetop for 3 minutes over high heat, then put into oven. Roast the birds until golden, about 15 minutes.

Serve the quail with the sauce on the side.

Elderflowers are a healthful pick-me-up in late spring. Their foraged blossoms can be made into a sweet sauce to accompany roasted quail.

SIDE DISHES

*Lavender-Scented Turnips,
Sunchokes, and Bacon*

MAKES 4 SERVINGS

Spicy, earthy turnips, nutty sunchokes, and salty bacon, sweet-ened by honey and lavender: a great side dish with steak or halibut. Sunchokes, a tuber in the sunflower family, are native to North America. Their flavor is reminiscent of artichokes, and they are available in the specialty produce section of your supermarket or at farmers markets. You could save the turnip tops, brown them in olive oil, and serve them alongside. If using mature turnips instead of baby turnips, be sure to peel them down to their tender flesh.

4 strips thinly sliced bacon or pancetta, cooked and
    crumbled (reserve fat)
4 sunchokes, peeled, finely diced, and placed in water
Kosher salt
Freshly ground black pepper
1 bunch (about 8) baby turnips, trimmed and quartered

1 tablespoon mild-flavored local honey

½ teaspoon dried lavender, pulverized

3 tablespoons white wine

In a small skillet, heat the bacon fat over medium heat. Add the sunchokes to the pan, along with salt and pepper to taste. Cook for a few minutes, until caramelized, then remove the sunchokes and reserve. Add the turnips to the pan and cook over medium heat until soft.

Increase the heat and stir in the honey, lavender, and white wine. Cook until the liquid is gone and the turnips are glazed and start to caramelize. Toss in the reserved sunchokes and crumbled bacon. Heat for 1 minute and serve warm.

Variations: Substitute Brussels sprouts for the turnips and nutmeg for the lavender.

Roasted Baby Pattypans with Lemon Verbena
MAKES 4 SERVINGS

The first baby pattypans are available at the farm in late spring. They are quite colorful and delicious roasted. Lemon verbena is available at specialty shops, farmers markets, and herb gardens.

1 pound whole baby pattypan squash

2 sprigs fresh lemon verbena

2 tablespoons olive oil

Kosher salt

Preheat the oven to 400 degrees F.

Home-cured bacon adds a smoky complexity to many dishes.

In a large mixing bowl, toss together the squash, lemon verbena, and olive oil. Spread the mixture on a rimmed baking sheet and add salt to taste. Roast in the oven about 12 minutes, until golden but slightly firm, stirring occasionally. Serve hot.

Tarragon-Spiked Carrots
MAKES 6 SERVINGS AS A GARNISH

This dish of sweet baby carrots infused with tarragon and a little white wine vinegar is a nice addition to a spring radish plate or salad. The carrots can accompany a hamburger, or just serve them as a pretty garnish on the plate. Rabbit bliss!

10 baby carrots, trimmed and quartered lengthwise

1 cup white wine or champagne vinegar

½ cup cold water

4 stalks of tarragon

Pinch of organic sugar (evaporated cane juice) or
       drizzle of honey

1 teaspoon kosher salt

Pinch of freshly ground black pepper

In a shallow pan, combine all ingredients. Refrigerate, covered, for 24 hours, tossing occasionally. Serve chilled or at room temperature.

DESSERTS

Rhubarb–Royal Anne Shortcakes with Licorice and Crème Fraîche
MAKES 6 SERVINGS

Royal Anne cherries are an old blush variety that is in danger of being lost. They are similar in nature to the Rainier cherry but slightly redder and a bit more tart. If you can't find Royal Anne cherries, substitute Rainier cherries.

Shortcakes:

- 1⅔ cups all-purpose flour
- 3½ tablespoons organic sugar (evaporated cane juice), plus more for topping
- 1½ tablespoons baking powder
- Pinch of kosher salt
- 8 to 12 tablespoons (1 to 1½ sticks) unsalted butter, cut into pieces
- ⅔ cup heavy cream, plus more for brushing tops of shortcakes
- Sugar or honey

Sauce and Topping:

- 1 cup organic sugar (evaporated cane juice)
- ½ cup water
- 4 stalks rhubarb, cut into ½-inch-thick slices
- 2 cups Royal Anne cherries, halved and pitted
- ¼ cup licorice- or anise-flavored liqueur
- 4 or 5 fresh peppermint leaves (optional)
- ½ cup crème fraîche

To prepare the shortcakes, preheat the oven to 350 degrees F.

In a food processor, mix the flour, evaporated cane juice, baking powder, and salt. Add the butter and pulse until the mixture

resembles a coarse meal. Stir in the heavy cream until just combined. Wrap the dough and chill in the refrigerator for 1 hour.

Roll the shortcake dough on a floured surface to a thickness
of 1 inch thick. Using the top of a juice glass, cut out 6 or
more circles. Place the cutouts on a parchment-lined baking
sheet, brush the tops with cream, and sprinkle each with a bit
of sugar or honey. Bake for 20 to 25 minutes, or until golden.
Cool briefly on the baking sheet.

To prepare the sauce, heat the sugar and water in a small
saucepan over medium-low heat until the sugar dissolves. Add
the rhubarb and simmer (do not stir) for about 3 minutes.
When the rhubarb appears soft, add the cherries, liqueur, and
peppermint. Simmer the mixture for another 3 to 4 minutes.
Remove from heat and cool briefly in the pan.

To assemble the shortcakes, slice each shortcake in half. Place
the bottom half on a plate and pour the sauce over. Add a
dollop of crème fraîche, then top with the other half.

Ricotta with Honey, Bee Pollen, and Blossoms
MAKES 4 SERVINGS

When fresh ricotta is at its prime, simple adornments let the
cheese show off. Hand-dipped ricotta is an artisanal method
of gently removing the curds to drain by hand. The resulting
ricotta is creamier and more flavorful than ricotta made with
mechanical methods. Bee pollen is available from your local
beekeeper and herbalist.

1 cup (about 8 ounces) fresh hand-dipped ricotta cheese
4 tablespoons mild-flavored local honey, such as wild-

*Rhubarb is often referred to as pie-plant; its acid tang
adds zip to spring treats like Rhubarb–Royal Ann Shortcakes with Licorice and Crème Fraîche.*

flower or fireweed
4 pinches of local bee pollen
Smattering of spring edible flowers, such as calendula petals, rosemary flowers, honeysuckle, pansies,
or fennel flowers

Divide the ricotta into 4 sherbet cups, drizzle with honey, and
top with bee pollen and flowers.

Variations: Substitute toasted hazelnuts, cherries, or the first
strawberries of the season for the flowers and pollen.

SPRING PANTRY

Chive-Blossom Vinegar
MAKES 4 CUPS

This pretty pink vinegar has a bit of bite—it's fabulous for
vinaigrettes, potato salad, and in fish marinades. Ask for chive
blossoms from herb vendors at your farmers market.

4 cups white wine vinegar
2 cups fresh chive blossoms

Pour the white wine vinegar into a large Mason jar. Add the
chive blossoms, then cap and let sit in a cool, dark place for
2 weeks. Strain the mixture and discard the chive blossoms.
Decant the vinegar into a quart jar or other vessel. Cap and
store in cool, dark pantry for up to 6 months.

Wild Rose Petal Jelly
MAKES 8 CUPS

This is a very pretty, delicate jelly for scones or biscuits. We
use verjus instead of lemon juice because it's available locally
and gives a nice grape undertone to the jelly. Verjus is available

bottled at specialty stores, some wineries, and grocers. Wild rose petals are available from your local forager. Commercial rose petals may be substituted only if they were not sprayed.

3½ pounds green apples, quartered

5 cups organic sugar (evaporated cane juice), divided

2 cups fresh wild rose petals

⅓ cup verjus or lemon juice

1 tablespoon rosewater, plus 1 teaspoon

Put the apples in a preserving pan or large stock pot with rack insert, cover with 6½ cups of water, and bring to a boil. Simmer for half an hour on medium-low heat. Pour the boiling

water and apples through a conical strainer lined with cheesecloth, pressing lightly on the fruit to release the juices. Chill the juice overnight.

The next day, remove 4½ cups of the juice, leaving the sediment in the bowl. Pour the juice in a preserving pan with 2-½ cups of the sugar. Add 1 cup of the rose petals to the pan and bring to a simmer. Remove from heat, transfer to a bowl, and reserve, covered with a cloth for 1 hour. Pour through a strainer lined with cheesecloth, pressing lightly on the rose petals.

Put this syrup in another preserving pan, add the verjus, and the remaining 2½ cups of sugar. Bring to a boil, stirring gently. Skim foam if needed. Continue cooking on high heat for 7 minutes, or until the jelly temperature has reached 221 degrees F. Add the rose water.

Divide the remaining rose petals among eight 8-ounce sterilized jelly jars, and pour the jelly into the jars. When the jelly is almost set, gently shake the jars so the rose petals are distributed.

Pie Cherry–Chile Jam
MAKES 4 PINT JARS

We love this delicious tart jam with a kick. Use as a base for chutney, add to sauces, or spread on toast. I suggest Montmorency, Morello, or Early Richmond cherry varieties for this jam.

6 pounds pitted sour cherries

6 cups organic sugar (evaporated cane juice)

2 dried arbol chiles

In a large mixing bowl, combine the cherries, sugar, and chiles and let the mixture sit in the refrigerator overnight. The next

A student examines a jar of raw snowberry honey.

An old homestead variety of rhubarb. Scattered around the valley, clumps of rhubarb mark the gardens of abandoned farms.

day, stir and mash the cherries and pour the mixture into a heavy-bottomed pot. Heat over medium heat, stirring occasionally until the liquid is thick and syrupy. Put into 4 sterilized pint jars and refrigerate for up to 2 months, or process in a hot water bath for 15 minutes for the pantry.

Spring Harvest List

Asparagus	Mâche
Baby lettuces	Pea vines
Baby vegetables	Peas
Cattails	Spinach
Fresh cheese	Spring onions
Green garlic	Wild mushrooms

SUMMER ABUNDANCE

SUMMER ABUNDANCE

IN JULY SUMMER IS IN FULL SWING. The garden is beginning to feel the sun ripening the foods that will sustain the farm's visitors throughout the year. This summer, toast might be topped with apricot preserves from last summer, even while the students are canning a new batch. The farm school is ready for its weeklong sessions of cooking, foraging, butchering, baking, preserving, curing, and more for fifteen to twenty chefs, food lovers, and potential farmers who make the trek from the city.

CITY KIDS ON THE FARM

An urban legend goes that a city gardener was working in his garden when some neighborhood kids stopped by. He showed them around and pulled a big orange carrot from the ground. One of the kids, astonished, said, "Whoa! How did you get *that* in there?"

Most of us, whether we are food lovers, avid home cooks, or even professional chefs, did not grow up on a farm. We love all things related to food, we love the idea of gardens and farms; but the fact is, most of us grew up buying our meat wrapped in plastic and our produce from large supermarkets, where it's displayed neatly under fluorescent lights, rather than from farm fields spread out under the sun, or even from farmers markets. This became a fact of contemporary urban life after World War II, with the rise of industrialized food production on a grand scale. The family farm began to die out in favor of large, industrialized one-crop farming operations. But this tide has started to ebb over the past few decades, with the rise of the organic movement, farmers markets, and even the Food Network.

"A whole channel just about food? It'll never work!" was many people's first reaction in 1993 when it premiered, but the Food Network is currently watched by millions around the world and has spawned countless imitators. Today, many Americans are obsessed with food. Whether the discussion is about childhood obesity and diabetes, transfats, GMOs, preservatives, food safety, fast food, so-called Frankenfoods, or regulations for raw milk, never in U.S. history have we had so many issues to deal with regarding food. Nor have we craved information about these issues so intensely.

Cherokee Purple tomato is listed by Slow Food USA, RAFT, and Ark of Taste. Once you taste a bite, you will know why.

One recent workshop at the farm school, "Developing a Food Culture and Sense of Place," brought a group of foodies together at Quillisascut to try their hand at goat milking, cheesemaking, herb infusions, and garden tending. The attendees included a homemaker from Spokane; a Seattle marketer and her fifteen-year-old daughter; a woman who works in the restaurant field and heads up a Slow Food convivium; a retired librarian and his son from Seattle; a Canadian who runs a furniture business near Bellingham; and Paul Haeder, a Spokane-based journalist who writes a sustainability column for *The Inlander*. Their reasons for attending the seminar were varied, but most folks said they wanted to learn about cooking with organic food and how to connect to the land where the food is grown.

Haeder's column captured these comments from workshop participants: "Alice Moravec from Spokane says she wants her five children to know the role food plays in their future and their own role in shaping their environment. 'This is the way it was for everyone to live just a few years ago,' she says. 'Everything is so fresh and pure.' And participant Tony Wilson, who recently retired as a librarian for Highline Community College, says the Quillisascut way is empowering. 'In my daily life, I breathe the air at night and consciously think how vital it is to breathe. It reestablishes me to the physical. Actually touching the stuff I eat makes it artistic and respectable.'"

The range of people drawn to the farm school shows how connected we all are. Another strong bond made at Quillisascut during the days before the school was developed, and continuing to the present, is between the Misterlys and personal chef Karl Vennes, formerly a cook at Rover's restaurant in Seattle and now a personal chef in a household where considerable corporate entertaining is required. Vennes got to know Rick and Lora Lea when they delivered cheese to the restaurant. "[Rick] always said, 'Come out and spend a few days,'" so a couple of years later, a road trip to eastern Washington found Vennes at the farm. "I spent ten days there, learning to make cheese, and have been going back every year. Rick was

The eight-foot-high woven wire garden fence keeps out goats as well as the native white-tailed deer.

learning at the time, too, so we kind of taught ourselves that way, by butchering a pig and making *jamón* and sausages and trying to learn how to use the whole animal."

Vennes feels the experience was something "most city chefs never get to do," and he's tried to put the philosophies he learned on the farm to use in his kitchen, essentially a grand home kitchen. Vennes's advice for home cooks: "Try not to be wasteful." Even if you have money, he says, it is satisfying to use everything you can from the food you buy.

He also spent some time in Spain, where he discovered the country's great cuisine and was particularly impressed by the different meats that don't usually appeal to American palates. "I fell in love with blood sausage," he says, which is made two ways in Spain—with onions and rice, or with lots of black pepper and rice. "Rick and I have made it and learned from various friends how to do it right." Vennes admits this is not something most Americans would do, but he says the process makes us aware that there is so much variety and possibility in the foods we use. "We should be adventurous in the kitchen," he says, "and try new things that we may just like after all."

TEACHING IN THE KITCHEN

The farm is the classroom, but the bunkhouse kitchen serves as HQ. The building is a long, straw-bale and stucco affair with a six-burner industrial stove and oven, a stained-concrete floor and countertops, and simple but beautiful wood cabinets that Rick and Lora Lea built, along with a dozen or so workers, friends, and tradespeople from the area. The bunkhouse kitchen is simple and inviting; it is both classroom and gathering place for the students who attend each session of the school. They meet here, around the sixteen-foot-long wooden table at the beginning of each day, to learn about different aspects of the farm's food systems, receive assignments, and share their experiences. The conversation is started with the "Word of the Day"—one word, such as "respect," "grateful," "seasonal," "community," or "enough"—that gets them thinking about the ways food impacts their lives, as they go through their daily farm chores and discover the life cycles of this place. While at the farm, the students also think about how they experience food and participate in their food systems at home.

Students pay close attention to details when fabricating a goat into smaller cuts.

Heirloom tomatoes: German Pink, Brandywine, Cherokee Purple, and Golden Oxheart

On the farm, teaching and eating go hand in hand. At the beginning of the day Chef Kären holds a meal-planning meeting, reviewing the current state of provisions—what is available, what meat has been recently slaughtered or cured, what melons or tomatoes or squash have been harvested, and so on. This morning the pantry is down to about eighteen eggs, so the plan is to make recipes with very few eggs in them for the next few days. A harvest list is created, and Kären takes the groups into the garden to show them what and how to harvest—how to tell what is ripe, how to pick something without damaging the plant, and then how to use what is in abundance at the right time.

"In early summer we work hard in the garden, and get mostly peas and greens. But then late summer comes, and we don't have to do much in the garden, just watch it grow and harvest," she says. Just looking out the kitchen window on a July day, you can see what she means: rows of beanstalks stretched up to shade the patio, pots of pear tomatoes starting to blush to pink and red, the dusty blue-green leaves of Romanesco broccoli promising the sculpted heads forming at their base. In the pantry, baskets full of melons—Charentais and Noirs des Carmes, Emerald Gem and Sweet Granite—fill the room with their earthy-sweet aroma. At this time of year the overriding question is what to do with all this abundance.

MAKING CHEESE

On the morning after a new group of visitors arrives, Lora Lea takes them to the cheesemaking demonstration kitchen to show them how to make cheese from that morning's goat's milk. She begins by heating the milk to 90 degrees Fahrenheit. Then she pours it into the cheese vat—a large stainless-steel tank that tips, so that later she can pour off the whey. Students watch as she adds the cheese culture, a bacterial strain that feeds on the lactose and converts it to lactic acid, lowering the pH and developing flavor. Next she adds rennet (an extract made from the inner lining of a calf's stomach used to curdle the milk), stirs it into the milk, and then lets the mixture rest for thirty minutes while the curdling process develops. At this point the milk is "set," or firm like a custard, and she cuts it into small cubes, called "curds." These contain the milk solids, and the leftover liquid—the whey—separates.

Lora Lea pours the whey into buckets, and now the students can get involved, carrying the buckets away and helping separate the curds into different containers for each of them to work with. "We save all this whey and give it to our friends at Paul's Pastured Poultry to feed their pigs," she says (see the farm profile on Paul's Pastured Poultry later in this chapter)

"just like the pigs in Parma that eat acorns and the whey left over from the cheesemaking process." Most of the students are surprised that the curd is very white and mild, with not much goaty flavor at all. "The flavors develop in the cheese during the aging process," Lora Lea explains. "Although every step of the cheesemaking process, from the feed the goats are eating to the climate of the aging cellar, is decided on and controlled by the cheesemaker, it is the mystery of it all that brings me to my senses when I take a bite of the ripened cheese." It is amazing

Opposite: Wheels of cheese line the shelves of the room where they are aged for two to six months.

Below: Fresh pressed curds are salted and air dried before being moved to the cheese cellar.

the difference even a week makes in this cheese. Today she is making her *curado*, a hard goat cheese aged for two months or more that is excellent for grating, made in eight-inch rounds and cut into smaller triangles when sold.

Lora Lea makes about five thousand pounds of cheese a year. The flavor and texture of the cheese varies throughout the year, as the qualities of the milk adjust to the seasonal diet of the goats. Temperature and day length also play a part. Since the goats are all on the same schedule in their lactation, the milk is changing for all of them. When they first "freshen" (that is, when they produce milk to feed their young), the milk is rich and creamy. As the summer progresses, the milk seems to have a higher water content. Fall and winter milk is higher in

Butchering: The Farmer's Perspective
by Rick Misterly, Quillisascut Farm School of the Domestic Arts

By the time a few days have passed on the farm, the chefs, students, and staff—all from different backgrounds and with different skill levels—invariably create a bond, an understanding of shared experiences that feels like family. But what brings us all together as a group? Is it the big, communal table where we sit and eat together each night? Is it the closeness of the bunkhouse quarters? Is it the work that we share in the garden and the kitchen? Or is it something else?

One activity that people say, more than any other, brings them closer, is butchering the larger animals. When we are ready to butcher a lamb or a goat, trepidation is palpable. Some people want no part of it, and others are eager to see this process. I consider myself the animals' caretaker—I've watched over them and fed them all their lives, and I know the care that has gone into their raising—as well as the intermediary between the animal and the students and chefs. So I feel a special responsibility, as both a human and a carnivore, to make butchering the animals as stress-free for the animals—and the humans—as possible.

First, I assure the students they will not see the actual death—except for chickens and ducks—because I feel that killing is not a spectator sport. My single biggest source of stress or uncertainty is how I can keep the animal as calm as possible. Being alone with the animal, and slaughtering it outdoors in the place where it was raised, is the best way to accomplish that.

About ten minutes after the animal's throat is slit, and I've hung it so that it bleeds out completely, the students see the animal still intact. Then the process of skinning and eviscerating begins. That's something most of these chefs, and most people in general, have never experienced. I encourage people to look at the animal, help remove the skin, and see how it feels. Students are surprised how clean the inside of an animal is—when slaughtering is done on this level, rather than in the large production-line slaughter facilities we hear about, it's not gory and bloody like something out of a horror movie.

Then we cut the animal in half. The thing that stands out is how neat and organized the inside of the animal is. I guess that is why they call them organs! We remove the organs that can be eaten—the heart, liver, the caul fat, and the testicles if the animal is male. We leave the kidneys inside the carcass until we break it down. An old butcher once told me this is the best way to do it, to protect the tenderloin and keep it full of blood—otherwise, it dries out. Then Chef Kären goes through the process of fabrication, or breaking the animal down into its different cuts and usable sections, and the students cook with these different parts of the animal, making everything from pâté to sausage to grilled tenderloin.

I feel this process is incredibly important, and that it draws us together because, in a way, we are all accomplices. Witnessing this process breaks down certain barriers. Some chefs come here with an aversion to seeing the death of an animal, but they still think it is important, so they overcome their fears with the rest of the group. They have seen the entire process, from the live state of the animal to enjoying the food on the plate. It is a primal experience and goes back into our human heritage, an understanding and an experience that on some level is missing from our lives today: understanding this cycle of life and death that connects us all.

fats and solids, and more of the pronounced goaty flavors come through in the cheese because of the fatty acids in the milk.

"The cheese I make is trying to give an honest reflection of all of those factors," Lora Lea says. "That is one of the biggest features of this or any artisan cheese. I want it to be an honest representation of this place. I want the cheese to be real, and full of rustic nuances. Even when it is mild, I want there to be lots of flavor." She continues: "I started out wanting to make a cheese that was like something I could buy at the store, except for the homemade cottage cheese like my Mom made. So that put it somewhere around Tillamook and Jarlsberg. Lucky for me, Rick always ate the cheese and said it was good, like something he tried in Greece or some other exotic locale. At some point I realized that there is a lot of industrialized cheese being made; what there is a shortage

When butchering, make sure to do the best job possible, show respect, and avoid waste by utilizing the entire animal.

of is simple honest farm-made cheese."

When Lora Lea started making cheese, using a recipe for Manchego, she thought it really clicked with her animals' milk, so she has stayed with that recipe over the years, modifying it a little to make it fit with the farm. "We call it 'curado' to reflect that early Spanish influence and separate it from the industrial imports." "I am always experimenting," she says. "This is my practice. I try to observe what is going on at so many levels. I pay attention to the way the milk and cheeses smell, the way things look, the way things feel to my hands, how they taste. Then I use my knowledge to control the information coming in. I think that is where the craftsmanship comes into play. And that is what we are trying to teach here on the farm."

FORAGING: A WILD FOOD WALK

Every session, Quillisascut students have a chance to get back to their primal hunter-gatherer roots. Even in this semiarid ecosystem, situated between the forest and the sagebrush

Hunting for ponderosa pine nuts on a foraging adventure at the farm

steppe of the upper Columbia River, it's easy to find many foods that grow wild. Today the students' wild food walk starts right in the driveway outside the bunkhouse. "Right behind the house here, you can find mallow, or buttonweed," Lora Lea says, as she reaches down to pick the roundish leaves of a common weed, even seen poking out of cracks in urban sidewalks. "This plant is related to hollyhocks and okra, and its texture is a little slimy." She unwraps a tiny button-shaped pod and hands out leaves for tasting. It tastes mild, and the texture is indeed slightly slimy but not unpleasant.

"Here's a pine nut," she says, picking one up from the driveway. The students crack it open and taste: a very piney, nutty, succulent flavor. "When we go on our walk, we want people to get to know the landscape. When the students go out, they get a sense of what the natural landscape really has to offer here, outside the protection of the gardens and the barns. Out on the road we find wild beaked hazelnuts, with their long husks, and in springtime down by the stream, we gather nettles and watercress and new cattail shoots that are down around the base of the plant. We sauté these like you would leeks."

In mid to late June the elderflowers, covered with their creamy white pollen, are an aromatic delicacy—one to enjoy until the berries are ripe in September and October. Along streambeds, mint and watercress are abundant, especially in late spring. And in the drier fields, Oregon grape, serviceberry (a dark blue berry with a large seed that tastes like almond, also called Saskatoon or juneberry), elderberry, and choke-cherries grow abundantly.

When does Chef Kären know to go out when the berries will be ready to pick? Around here, Lora Lea explains, this

Butchering: A Student's Perspective
by Joanna Moogk, Seattle Culinary Academy Student

We had butchered the lamb earlier that week and broken down the carcass. I think I was still in awe from the whole experience—how many beginning culinary students, or chefs for that matter, have the chance to witness this process from start to finish? How many professional cooks get to fabricate an entire carcass, actually seeing firsthand where every cut of meat originates? How many people recognize that the whole process—when done with tenderness, respect, and skill—is unbelievably clean and uncannily beautiful? It was the last thing I expected.

When I read "6:00 AM—Butcher lamb" on the agenda for the second day at the Quillisascut Farm School, I felt uneasy. I was looking forward to milking goats. I was looking forward to making cheese. I was looking forward to harvesting fresh produce from the gardens and cooking amazing meals. I was even looking forward to a lecture about composting. I was not looking forward to butchering a lamb. Who would? Lambs are cute and fuzzy, and I wasn't so sure I was prepared to get emotionally attached to my dinner. Was it so wrong to just purchase a beautiful rack from the butcher and get enough satisfaction from frenching the bones to perfection (cutting away the meat and fat to make a beautiful presentation), without actually seeing its gentle eyes and soft wool? Of course it's not wrong, and it's the most practical option for most of us carnivorous city-dwellers. But there is one thing I am absolutely sure of:

that the meat from that lamb was the best dinner I have ever eaten in my life, and the meal satisfied much more than just my belly.

Twelve new friends sat around a cozy table and had the feast of our lives: a crudité platter harvested straight from the garden, overflowing with baby eggplant, tender haricots verts, four rosy shades of beets, perfect fingerling potatoes, and a rainbow of heirloom tomatoes, accompanied by fromage blanc straight from the goats we had risen so early to milk; poblano chiles stuffed with home-grown potatoes and "No-Name" Quillisascut cheese (the nameless curado that was so delicious—it became famous to us in spite of its missing identity); olive–thyme *levain* that had been freshly baked in a wood-burning oven that doubled as a warm bench for after-dinner stargazing; and of course, the main course, a perfectly grilled rack of lamb. Practically everything that was on the table had originated on the farm. We had come in direct contact with every morsel that was going into our bodies that night. No meal had ever felt so complete.

I get goose bumps when I think back to that dinner in particular and the farm school experience as a whole. Nothing has ever changed my life in such a tangible and succinct way. I was able to walk away with conviction and direction, passion and motivation. Sitting down to a meal and truly experiencing the philosophy of "farm to table" is magical, even if it means getting emotionally attached to the main course.

A Lesson in Stillness
by Chef David Blaine, Latah Bistro, Spokane, Washington

Riding my bike up the gravel driveway of Quillisascut Farm, I was aware of the tranquility that I was disturbing. The sound of the rocks under my tires and the rapid huffing and puffing of my breathing were in contrast to the stillness of the natural world around me. The stillness is not motionlessness. The dogs were ambling down to meet me, a hawk was circling above, looking for a morning meal, and the goats were working their way through the lower pasture. The stillness is calm; it is the smooth assured way that nature goes about its business, the calm that permeates the people who choose to *follow* nature rather than *change* it.

Throughout my time at Quillisascut, I found that the lessons we were learning were born of this peace. Picking peaches fast was not as important as picking them when they were ready to be picked. The process of butchering the goat was built around respecting the animal's role in the natural order. Baking bread required forgetting about other activities that were going on and focusing on the components that come together to make grain into food, using only what comes from water and the air.

The final lesson of my time at the school is practiced every day. With the natural world enveloping you from every side, it is easy to find yourself carried away in the calm. Amid the stainless steel and brick, under fluorescent lights, surrounded by the noisy city, I slow my breath, close my eyes, find my calm, and look for ways to respect nature as it comes to me in the unnatural environment of my kitchen. If haste makes waste, then calm finds solutions for the excess of a busy kitchen and a busy life. Calm reconnects cooking to both the eating and the growing. Calm allows for creativity that never loses the origins of the food. Finding calm has been a way to keep alive the passion for my craft that I rediscovered in the stillness of Quillisascut Farm.

is communal knowledge among people who have wandered these fields for years, observing their surroundings and learning through trial and error. "We make sure we don't pick everything." She describes the elderflowers she gathers, long bunches laden with pollen. "We infuse these in a simple syrup, and you can use them in various drinks and sauces; they have a very lovely floral aroma."

Rose hips are all over the place, too. These hard, red nubs are what is left when the rose petals fall off, and the hips should be bright red, not orange, when they are ready. They are edible by themselves, although they're pithy and full of little seeds. But they have a nice citrusy, floral flavor, which is stronger when they've been cooked down or dried for tea or infusions.

Oregon grape, a small round berry, grows abundantly in many landscaped city gardens, and here at the farm it's ubiquitous: a low bush with a prickly holly-shaped leaf and smooth bluish-purple berries with a powdery-white bloom. You can add sugar to these tannic berries to make a flavorful syrup or jelly. Ranging just a few hundred yards from the house, the students fill their bags with berries, mint, watercress, and Oregon grape. When they return to the bunkhouse kitchen, they pour everything out on the table and separate it into bowls, each person thinking of what delicacies will be created.

BAKING IN THE WOOD-FIRED OVEN

Several bakers, including Don Reed (pastry instructor at the Seattle Culinary Academy at Seattle Central Community College, who helped set up the wood-burning oven outside on the patio behind the bunkhouse) and Lynda Oosterhuis (a baker for Café Juanita in Kirkland, Washington), come to the farm with a mission: to bake as many loaves of bread as they can in one day. Lynda currently farms in southern Oregon in summer, is a mercenary pastry chef in Seattle, and is a frequent guest baker here at Quillisascut. She makes beautiful bread, for which we are most grateful. When Oosterhuis bakes, she likes to get started early, waking up with the roosters and building a fire in the oven. The dough for the bread has been prepared the day before and is waiting in the walk-in cooler. She takes time to have a cup of coffee, enjoy the sunrise, and watch the

The wood-fired oven is a versatile tool for baking and braising; it also slows us down and connects us with the primal energy of fire.

wild turkeys in the lower field. "Morning has always been my favorite time of day," she says, "when smells and sounds are much clearer. My only job is to maintain the fire, allowing the heat to collect in the massive walls of the brick and stucco oven." It may take up to five hours for the oven to get enough heat stored up to bake bread.

Oosterhuis hopes her calculations and timing are correct and that the rising bread will be ready just when the oven reaches optimum temperature. If she starts early, she can bake three batches of bread—almost thirty loaves—plus fruit tarts, cookies, and other goodies. She's prepared for days for this—creating the doughs, feeding starters, gathering cherries, and harvesting a few pounds of wheat that she planted just for this purpose and then threshing and grinding it. The grains and flours she uses are usually a combination of the wheat harvested on the farm, wheat flour from Shepherd's Grain (a wheat-farming cooperative in eastern Washington), and rye from Bluebird Grains (in the Methow Valley in north-central Washington).

"Baking on the farm is a very different experience from baking in a restaurant," says Oosterhuis, who has baked in kitchens around Seattle since the late 1990s. "There is no loud music, no mixers, no knobs to turn or buttons to push. It is more splintery fingers from stoking the fire, and dough-covered hands, guiding along the fermentation process, with the wild yeasts in the air, allowing time to do most of the work." She finds great satisfaction in pulling out crusty golden loaves from the oven, "knowing that I have created something truly of this place." Everyone can smell the loaves and everyone is impatient to slice into one, spreading homemade jams on the hot, aromatic bread.

Oosterhuis sees baking as the essence of what Quillisascut Farm is all about—gathering grains, fruits, and nuts from the fields and gardens, then creating these delicious loaves to share

Daily chores for restaurant staff attending a farm retreat are posted, with the day starting at 5:30 AM.

with the others who are here, who have been working hard on their own projects all day. The simple act of creating delicious food and sharing it with others is what she calls a "true picture of what a food community looks like."

EATING TOGETHER: UNDERSTANDING THE DAY

After a full day of work and discovery at Quillisascut Farm, the dinner crew is in full swing. The menu is written neatly on a chalkboard: pan-roasted duck breast with chokecherry jus, baked potatoes stuffed with lamb kidneys, Alicia's "Rooty" slaw, braised red cabbage with caraway, salad of green beans and mint, and zucchini cake with mascarpone cheese frosting. This might be some little French country bistro, and it bustles with activity as cooks work on their creations. One student chops mint, filling the room with its fresh, earthy aroma;

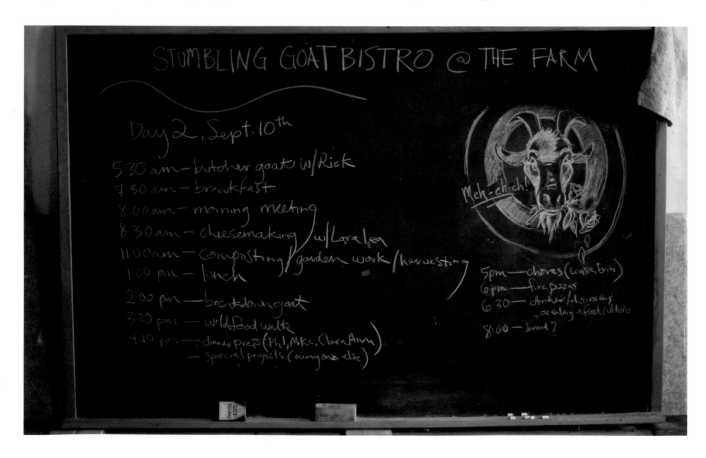

This Ain't No Chick-Fil-A
by Chef Becky Selengut, www.seasonalcornucopia.com

Becky Selengut, chef and founder of the seasonal foods website www.seasonalcornucopia.com, which has become popular with chefs and farmers, kept a journal during her stay at Quillisascut Farm that captures the lively experience of butchering her first chicken.

5:45 AM: This ain't no Chick-fil-A. So it's chicken-butchering time here on the farm and back home at this time I'd be hours from waking up. Regardless, here I am handing over ten-pound-plus chickens to Rick as he lays them down over a two-by-four, and while his left hand holds them by the legs, his right swings the hatchet. (Skip ahead if you're faint of stomach.) I had always heard that chickens still move around when they lose their heads. But I imagined that to mean some reflexive movements, sort of subtle-like. Lesson one: Chickens go freakin' crazy. Head off, Rick holding its feet, the chicken is flapping its wings full force for a disturbing minute, at least. Okay, lesson two: If you unintentionally (or later, intentionally) press down on a chicken's cavity when plucking it, it can cackle aloud just like a live chicken. Apparently, its voice box (or voice box equivalent) does not need a head to function. This happened inadvertently to someone's chicken on the table where we were working, and we all jumped back in horror!

We dip the chickens in scalding hot water to loosen the feathers and set to pluckin' them (which takes a really long time). Whereas the lamb is very clean to butcher, the chicken is dirty, dirty, dirty. The only real way to remove all the internal organs is just to dig them out carefully with your hands, trying really hard not to puncture the intestines. I am treated to an unexpected surprise when I pull my hand out and see two small oval sacs. "What are these?" "Oh, great! Those are chicken balls. They're a tasty delicacy," says Rick. Later, I fry them up in butter and learn another important lesson: Always poke a small hole in each chicken testicle before you fry them. Basically they just got bigger and tighter in the pan until I exploded them, spraying hot butter all over myself and anyone within a ten-foot radius. What was left was certainly tasty, though.

Meanwhile, Jet, the puppy, runs back and forth with a chicken head in her mouth.

another stirs one of several pots bubbling away on the stove.

Finally, we sit down to eat, with the bounty and the lessons of the day spread out on the table. The students have become farmers and chefs today, and they talk about what has brought them here, what they have learned. "For a lot of people, it is seeing the farm and learning about food connections," intern Kate Posey says. "For me, though, it is seeing the people that are here—not only the inspired cooking that happens with this fabulous perfect produce, but the animal husbandry, the butchering is new to me. So it is really exciting to be on a highly diversified small farm, seeing it all together."

When the chefs prepare to leave, inevitably they talk about plans—what they might do upon their return to the city and the new connections they will keep. Posey says, "The farm is a place to dream about the ways we can use the skills learned here, with a new level of respect for ingredients and the process and people behind the growing and raising of foods."

Farm Profile: Paul's Pastured Poultry
Paul Dye and Susan Lieberman, Rice, Washington

Paul Dye and Susan Lieberman bought their farm near Rice, Washington, on eBay in 2004. They had retired in Michigan and knew that they wanted to become farmers, but they weren't sure what they wanted to raise. A class at their local university extension program gave them a direction, and the happenstance of finding this farm for sale gave them the push they needed to pull up stakes and move to Stevens County.

They also knew they wanted to "walk this earth with as small a footprint as possible." Their first project, begun in 2005, was raising free-range poultry, and they have since added turkeys, pigs, and Scottish Highland cattle to their farm. Their goal, they say, is to "provide friends and neighbors with naturally raised, great-tasting poultry," and they've done that—the Misterlys often buy Paul and Susan's chickens, keeping their own hens for eggs.

Starting out with classic Cornish Crosses, they've also branched out to lesser-known hybrid chicken breeds, such as the red Bronze Ranger that does better on pasture than the Cornish Cross and the mottled Grey Ranger with its barred black and white feathers. For their chickens they use "chicken tractors"—bottomless, portable pens that let the birds range. The pens are moved often, to new grassy areas, giving the chickens fresh food and helping avoid exposure to bacteria and disease. This method helps to fertilize the fields or vineyards as well. Paul and Susan have been using the pens for two years, and they are "amazed at the improvement of the quality" of their fields, which now are "lush and almost weed free."

They also got excited about raising turkeys but found that "the poultry factories had made hybrid, confinement-raised turkeys so cheap to buy—never mind your health—that the older breeds have nearly become extinct." So they researched and obtained three breeds of heritage birds through the National Livestock Breeds Conservancy: the beautiful black, grey, tan, and white Narragansett, a cross between native turkeys and European domesticated birds; the deep rust-colored Bourbon Red, developed from the Buff turkey in Kentucky, Ohio, and Pennsylvania; and the White Holland, which is thought to have originated in the New World and been transported to Europe in the 1500s. Seattle chef Tom Douglas recently invited Paul and Susan to bring their birds to a turkey tasting at his Dahlia Lounge restaurant. "The results were unanimous," says Paul. "The heritage breeds were superior in taste and texture to the commercially raised birds."

Paul and Susan are great examples of farmers who have rejected industrialized farming methods in favor of sustainable practices. Their organic, humanely raised meat and poultry not only are better for the animal and the conscience but provide more delicious meat as well—not to mention being far more healthy for us all.

The Stumbling Goat temporarily closed its doors to send the staff to a sustainable kitchen retreat at Quillisascut. One staff member puts the finishing touches on a fresh vegetable salad.

SUMMER
RECIPES

THE KITCHEN AT QUILLISASCUT FARM is busy in summer, the growing season. The students come and inspire us to create new recipes. We experiment with leek flowers; forage for watercress and huckleberries; relish apricots, then peaches, then plums. Tomatoes begin to ripen; cucumbers, eggplant, chiles, Provider beans, and summer squash fill us up. The first sweet corn and its fungal friend huitlacoche put us in the mood for tamales. Foods are simpler now, the flavors at their peak, they need no dressing up; peaches are best eaten just off the tree with the juices running down your arm. The canning process is in full swing as we attempt to capture summer flavors to brighten our taste buds in the darker seasons. Summer is the buildup to harvest, the turning point that throws us into fall.

Fresh cheese, preserved jams, and bread make a filling summer breakfast.

BREAKFAST & BREADS

Apricot–Grilled Cheese Breakfast Sandwiches
MAKES 4 SERVINGS

Inspired by fresh baguettes from our wood-fired oven, this breakfast treat tastes better than candy. The method is similar to a typical grilled-cheese sandwich, but we have used tangy goat cheese and sweet, tart apricot preserves.

1 baguette, about 20 inches long and 3 to 4 inches thick
½ cup Apricot Preserves (recipe follows in the "Summer Pantry" section)
½ cup fresh chèvre
4 tablespoons (½ stick) unsalted butter

Cut a baguette in half lengthwise, then trim off the crusty top of each piece and reserve for another use. Cut each half lengthwise into 4 long slices (you will have 8 slices total). Spread 4 of the slices liberally with apricot preserves, and spread the other 4 slices with fresh chèvre. Sandwich together and butter the tops and bottoms.

Heat a large skillet and fry the sandwiches until golden, turning once. Serve hot.

Variation: Any preserves substitution would be delicious.

SOUPS & SALADS

Yin-Yang Melon Soup
MAKES ABOUT 10 SERVINGS

Sweet, cooling melon on a hot summer day! This soup is not filling, so it makes a great starter course for a garden lunch. To create the unique presentation, you will need two pitchers for serving. Depending on the size and ripeness of the melons, you may need to adjust the amount of half-and-half. If the melons are very large, consider using only half. The consistency should be that of heavy cream, although a little thinner will work provided both soups are the same density.

    4 cups half-and-half, divided
    2 tablespoons lavender flowers
    2 tablespoons chopped spearmint leaves
    1 Charentais melon (or cantaloupe), seeded, skinned,
        and cut into small pieces
    Kosher salt
    1 small honeydew melon, seeded, skinned, and
        cut into small pieces

Divide the half-and-half between two small saucepots. Put the

Refreshing chilled soups are an inspired way to use the garden's harvest on a hot day.

lavender flowers in one and the spearmint leaves in the other. Bring both pots to a scald, until the milk just bubbles on the side of the pan. Then remove from heat and let steep for 10 minutes. Strain each, reserve, and chill.

In a food processor or blender, purée the Charentais. Add the lavender crème until smooth and season with salt to taste. Pour into a pitcher and reserve. Next, purée the honeydew, add the spearmint crème, and season with salt to taste. Pour into another pitcher and reserve.

Pour into each serving bowl from both pitchers at the same time. The soups should meet in the center. Garnish with spearmint leaves and lavender buds.

Seasonal variations: If you make this soup with watermelon, use heavy cream instead of half-and-half, since puréed watermelon is much thinner. Any herb can be substituted for the lavender and spearmint.

Heirloom Tomatoes and Frizzled Peppers with Sweet Corn–Marjoram Vinaigrette

MAKES 6 SERVINGS

Sweet, tangy, spicy, and colorful! We love this dish for dress-up occasions, when we don't just eat our heirlooms with salt.

Peppers:

1½ cups vegetable oil for frying (depending on size of saucepan)

4 to 6 small mild-to-spicy fresh peppers (such as jalapeños, turkish hots, or serranos), seeded and thinly sliced

2 garlic cloves, thinly sliced

Kosher salt

Vinaigrette (makes 2½ cups):

 2 cups fresh corn kernels (cut from about 4 to 6 ears) and
    corn milk scraped from the cobs

 1 tablespoon fresh chopped marjoram leaves

 1 teaspoon minced shallot

 ⅓ cup white wine vinegar

 ⅔ cup organic canola oil

 Kosher salt

 Pinch of freshly ground black pepper

Tomatoes:

 4 to 6 heirloom tomatoes of various sizes and colors,
    trimmed and sliced

 A handful of cherry tomatoes, sliced in half

To prepare the peppers, heat 2 inches of vegetable oil in a small saucepan over medium heat, until the oil ripples slightly. Add the peppers in batches and fry for about 5 minutes, or until soft, wrinkled, and lightly browned.

Remove peppers with a slotted spoon and put in a bowl. Add the garlic and a generous pinch of salt. Toss gently, then let the mixture rest for 10 minutes. (Reserve the oil for another use. It will be spicy; use it for sautéing, in vinaigrettes, or as a dip for bread and crudités.)

To make the vinaigrette, purée the corn kernels and corn milk, marjoram leaves, shallot, white wine vinegar, canola oil, salt, and pepper in a blender until smooth. Adjust seasonings if necessary.

Arrange the tomatoes on a serving plate. Sprinkle with salt to taste, top with the reserved vinaigrette, then garnish liberally with fried peppers.

A tomato salad shows off a variety of shapes and colors fit for a queen.

Huitlacoche Soup with Squash Blossoms
MAKES 8 SERVINGS

Huitlacoche is an exotic fungus that grows on corn. It's highly prized in Mexico, and we find it on about 10 percent of our corn crop. It is inky black in color and has a nutty corn flavor and an earthy hint of mushroom. It takes on the somewhat starchy characteristic of corn, so this soup will thicken as it cools. If the soup gets too thick before serving, simply thin with water.

To harvest or buy huitlacoche (also known as the corn mushroom), look for firm texture; the fungus should be from the ears of the corn, not the stalks. Trim any frayed black ends from the fungus. You will find huitlacoche—fresh, frozen, and often dried—at farmers markets, Latino markets, and specialty grocers. Huitlacoche can be frozen; just trim away any bits of corn cob or frayed ends. If frozen, however, it will be unattractive and should be used only in recipes that will feature the ingredient puréed.

When selecting zucchini blossoms, look for the male flowers, as they are generally smaller at the base than the females. The female blossoms have the beginnings of a baby squash at their base.

 4 tablespoons (½ stick) unsalted butter

 1 sweet onion, chopped

 5 cloves garlic, finely chopped

 4 cups chopped fresh huitlacoche

 4 cups chicken or vegetable stock

 1 tablespoon cumin seeds, toasted and ground

 1 dried arbol chile, whole

 Kosher salt

 8 male zucchini blossoms

 8 to 10 cherry tomatoes, chopped

 ½ cup fresh chèvre

 Olive oil

Preheat the oven to 325 degrees F.

In a large stockpot, melt the butter over medium heat. Stir in the sweet onion, garlic, and huitlacoche. Sauté for about 8 to 10 minutes, or until the mixture softens. Add the stock, cumin, and chile. Simmer, covered, over low heat for 20 minutes.

Remove the chile and purée the soup. Return puréed soup to the stockpot and season to taste with salt. Set the cover askew and keep warm over low heat.

Pinch the stamen from the center of each zucchini blossom. Mix the tomatoes with the chèvre and season with salt to taste. Stuff the blossoms with the tomato-chèvre mixture and close them. Put the blossoms on a baking sheet and brush with oil. Bake for 10 minutes, or until the chèvre is soft.

To serve, pour the soup into individual bowls and top with a stuffed blossom.

ENTRÉES

Roasted Chile and Cornmeal Tart
MAKES 8 SERVINGS

This recipe is adapted from Rosie Ramirez, who has attended the Quillisascut Farm School as both a student and as our kitchen sous-chef. She is our authority on all things Mexican. Rosie taught us how to clean our pots with ashes and how to use a broom like you mean it. She also taught us about chiles. Our garden abounds with many varieties of chiles, thanks to Rosie and her prince Antonio.

Verjus is made from the pressing of unripened grapes. It is available in specialty stores, farmers markets, and wineries.

Crust:

  1¼ cups all-purpose flour

  1 cup yellow cornmeal

  1 teaspoon baking powder

  4 tablespoons (½ stick) cold unsalted butter,
      cut into pieces

  2 cups fresh corn kernels (from about 2 to 3 ears)

  1 tablespoon verjus or lemon juice

  3 tablespoons sour cream

  Kosher salt

Marinated chiles:

  2 cloves garlic, crushed

  1 teaspoon fresh thyme

  ¼ cup chopped fresh oregano

  1 cup chopped fresh basil

  1 teaspoon kosher salt

  2 tablespoons olive oil

  8 roasted poblano chiles, peeled, seeded,
      and thinly sliced

Filling:

  2 pounds ripe heirloom tomatoes, sliced, salted, and
      drained (reserve juice for another use)

  3 cups (about 12 ounces) shredded Quillisascut Smoked
      Curado cheese or other smoked cheese

Preheat the oven to 375 degrees F.

To prepare the crust, mix together the flour, cornmeal, and baking powder in a large bowl. Cut in the butter, mixing by hand, until the mixture resembles small white peas.

In a blender, purée the corn kernels, verjus, and sour cream. Season with salt to taste. Combine with the butter-flour-cornmeal mixture until a dough forms (dough may be sticky).

White Sonoran corn gets a hug from a Sivri Biber pepper.

Refrigerate 1 hour.

Roll the dough on a floured surface to a thickness of ¼ inch, into a round about 10 inches in diameter. Press into an 8-inch tart pan. Refrigerate until ready to use.

Prepare the marinade for the chiles, by mixing together the garlic, thyme, oregano, basil, salt, and oil in a glass dish. Marinate the chiles in the mixture for 20 minutes.

To prepare the filling, layer the tomatoes, marinated chiles, and the cheese in a dough-lined pan, alternating until all are used. Fold the edges of the dough over the filling edge about 1 inch, leaving the center open. Bake for 45 minutes, or until the crust is golden and the center of the tart is set.

Handkerchief Pasta with Ruby Beets, Rainbow Chard, and Chervil

MAKES 4 SERVINGS

This dish of colorful, light vegetarian pasta contrasts earthy beets and greens. The ricotta salata adds a pungent kick. Fresh chervil is quite delicate, so it's best when picked just before using. If you aren't lucky enough to have it growing at your doorstep, you will find it in your produce section; select chervil with bright green leaves and a delicate anise scent.

4 medium ruby red beets, trimmed

Kosher salt

½ cup (1 stick) unsalted butter

Freshly cracked black pepper

2 shallots, minced

2 cloves garlic, minced

16 large rainbow chard leaves (leaves chopped, stems finely diced)

½ cup white wine

12 squares of uncooked fresh pasta, each about 4 inches square

¼ cup (about 20 ounces) crumbled ricotta salata, plus 4 tablespoons for garnish

½ cup chopped chervil and fronds for garnish

Drizzle of extra virgin olive oil

Sneaking a taste of a Jacob's Cattle bean during the fall harvest

Preheat the oven to 400 degrees F.

Place the beets in a shallow baking dish or ovenproof skillet. Pour in water about halfway up the level of the beets, and add a sprinkling of kosher salt. Cover. Put in the oven and roast until fork-tender, about 40 minutes. Remove and cool the beets in the dish until ready to handle, then peel, dice, and reserve.

Set some salted water to boil for the pasta. In a saucepan, melt 1 tablespoon of the butter and add the reserved beets. Toss and heat just through, and season to taste with salt and pepper. Set cover askew and keep warm over low heat.

In a large sauté pan, melt 2 tablespoons of the butter over medium heat. Cook the shallots, garlic, and chard stems until soft, about 3 minutes. Add 2 more tablespoons of butter. After the butter melts, stir in the chard leaves and cook gently for about 3 minutes, or until soft. Season with salt, then stir in 2 more tablespoons of butter and the white wine. Cook the mixture for about 5 more minutes.

Meanwhile, cook the pasta for 3 to 4 minutes, until al dente. Drain and toss the pasta with the remaining butter.

Assemble the dish in 4 wide soup bowls. Begin with a layer of the chard mixture, then lay a pasta square on the mixture and fill with more of the chard mixture and beets. Sprinkle on some ricotta salata and a bit of chervil and top with another pasta square. Repeat this process with filling and a third pasta square. Top with beets, ricotta salata, and pan drippings from the chard. Drizzle with olive oil and freshly cracked black pepper. Garnish with chervil fronds and the remaining ricotta salata. Serve immediately.

Variations: Make your own fresh pasta dough and color it with beet or carrot juice for an even more vibrant presentation.

Spit-Roasted Pastured Chicken with Chimichurri
MAKES 4 SERVINGS

Roasting chicken on the outdoor rotisserie is a great way to keep the heat out of the kitchen when the summer heat is on, although you can roast it in the oven as well. Chimichurri is the Argentine answer to pesto. It is best made the day before you plan to use it, so the flavors can blend and mellow.

Brine:

    8 cups water
    2 cups kosher salt
    1 cup brown sugar
    1 cinnamon stick
    2 tablespoons cumin seed
    2 dried chipotle chiles
    1 tablespoon coriander seeds, whole
    3 fresh or dried bay leaves
    8 cups ice water

    1 pasture-raised chicken, trussed
    Olive oil for basting

Chimichurri:

    1 head garlic, cloves peeled and crushed
    6 to 8 fresh serrano chiles, seeded and minced
    1 cup finely chopped fresh flat-leaf parsley
    2 cups finely chopped fresh cilantro
    ½ cup red wine vinegar
    1 tablespoon kosher salt

To prepare the brine, heat the water, salt, brown sugar, cinnamon stick, cumin, chiles, coriander, and bay leaves in a large stockpot over medium-high heat. Steep the brine for 15 minutes. Remove from the stovetop and pour the brine into a container large enough to hold the chicken, brine, and ice water. Pour in the ice water.

When the brine is cool, add the chicken, cover, and refrigerate 4 hours or overnight. *Note:* The brine mixture must be cool before adding the chicken, so refrigerate if necessary.

To prepare chimichurri, mix the garlic, serrano chiles, parsley, cilantro, red wine vinegar, and salt. Purée the mixture and let rest overnight in the refrigerator.

When you are ready to roast the chicken, remove it from the brine and pat dry. Place the chicken on the rotisserie and cook, basting with olive oil a few times, for roughly 90 minutes or until the internal temperature reaches 165 degrees F. (To check the temperature, insert a thermometer between the thigh and the breast; when the thermometer is removed, the juices should run clear.)

Carve the chicken, serve with chimichurri on the side.

Variation: If you don't have access to a rotisserie, roast the chicken in an oven preheated to 400 degrees F. Melt some bacon or other fat in a heavy cast-iron skillet on the stovetop. Put the chicken breast side down in the skillet, place in the oven, and cook for 20 minutes. Reduce the heat to 350 degrees, then turn the chicken breast side up and cook for 30 minutes more, or until the internal temperature reaches 165 degrees F.

Grilled Karakul Lamb Loin in Grape Leaves with Tomato Jam
MAKES 6 SERVINGS

Karakul lamb is a Central Asian heritage breed of lamb that is at home in the dry hills of Eastern Washington. The lamb wears its fat on the outside of the meat, so the cuts are very lean. This dish flirts with Middle Eastern flavors, smoke, warm spices, and a touch of heat. Grilling the loins briefly and then finishing them in a low oven prevents the grape leaves from burning off the meat.

Tomato jam:

    2 cups chopped Oxheart tomatoes (or other
        heirloom variety)
    2 dried arbol chiles, whole
    4 whole cardamom pods
    2 whole star anise pods
    ¼ teaspoon whole cloves
    ½ teaspoon cracked peppercorns
    1 fresh or dried bay leaf
    ½ cup organic sugar (evaporated cane juice)
    ¼ cup cider vinegar
    Salt

Lamb:

    ½ teaspoon toasted and ground cumin seeds
    ¼ teaspoon ground cardamom
    2 tablespoons kosher salt
    Freshly cracked pepper
    1½ pounds boneless Karakul (or other breed) lamb loins
    About 16 fresh grape leaves, blanched (or jarred leaves,
        well rinsed)
    Olive oil for grilling

To prepare the tomato jam, cook the tomatoes in a large saucepot over medium heat until liquefied. Add the chiles, cardamom pods, star anise pods, cloves, peppercorns, and bay leaf. Cook until reduced by about one-third. Stir in the sugar and cider vinegar, and continue cooking until the sauce coats the back of a spoon. Strain and discard the spices. Season with salt to taste. The sauce should have a tart, sweet, peppery taste. Reserve and keep warm.

To prepare the lamb, mix the cumin seeds, cardamom, salt, and cracked pepper in a small bowl. Rub the lamb with the spice mixture. Lay the grape leaves on a cutting board, overlapping each other. Place the lamb loins on the grape leaves and wrap the leaves around each loin individually, leaving no gaps. Use olive oil to seal if necessary. Brush liberally with olive oil.

Preheat the oven to 400 degrees F and heat grill over medium-high heat or coals. Grill the loins, 2 to 3 minutes per side, turning once. There should be crisp, distinct grill marks on each side.

Place the grilled loins on a baking sheet and finish cooking in the oven, for about 7 minutes, until the internal temperature is 135 degrees. Let the loins rest at least 5 minutes before cutting. Slice across the grain and serve with tomato jam.

SIDE DISHES

Aunt Molly's Ground Cherries, Godiva Style

MAKES 1 SERVING (OR 2 IF SHARED WITH A FRIEND)

Lora Lea developed this recipe using ground cherries, also known as Cape Cod gooseberries. These particular ground cherries are RAFT listed. They resemble a tomatillo in that they have a little husk to peel back. When they ripen to a deep yellow or amber-pink and drop to the ground, they are incredibly sweet-tart. They are so delicious that we never get around to using them in recipes. Perhaps they would make a nice clafouti or pie? We are not sure because we have never tried.

    1 ground cherry patch

Search under the ground cherry bush for the pinkish-yellow husks, peel back the husk, and pop them in your mouth. Repeat until the sun gets too hot or the curds need to be stirred. Gather a few more to share with your friend.

Variation: Have your *friend* go to the ground cherry patch.

Sweet Corn, Summer Squash, and Squash-Blossom Tamales

MAKES ABOUT 30 SMALL TAMALES

Although we give a recipe for fresh masa dough here, you can purchase fresh masa at a Latino grocery or dried masa flour at most supermarkets. Look for organic corn to avoid genetically modified corn. In Native American and Latin American cooking, calcium hydroxide is called "cal." Corn cooked with cal becomes *nixtamal,* which significantly increases its nutritional value and is also considered tastier and easier to digest. Cal lime is available at pharmacies and Latino markets, as are flour corn and dried corn husks.

Small tamales wrapped in fresh corn husks are ready for steaming.

Masa dough:

2 tablespoons cal lime

1½ pounds dry organic flour corn

8 cups water

Tamale dough:

1¼ cups lard

2 teaspoons kosher salt

1 teaspoon organic or GMO-free baking powder

1½ pounds fresh masa dough or rehydrated masa (3½ cups dry masa flour mixed with 2½ cups water)

1 cup chicken stock

2 cups fresh sweet corn kernels (cut from 2 to 3 ears)

Filling:

    1 tablespoon unsalted butter

    1 medium summer squash, diced (about 4 cups)

    ¼ teaspoon ground cayenne

    Salt and pepper

    ½ cup (about 4 ounces) fresh goat cheese, such as chèvre

    10 squash blossoms, finely cut

    70 fresh corn husks (from about 12 ears), or corn leaves, or dried husks rehydrated

To make the masa dough, dissolve the cal lime in a large stockpot with the water by stirring briefly. Add the flour corn, and bring the mixture to a boil for 2 minutes. Let soak refrigerated overnight. The next day, drain and rinse corn thoroughly. Grind the corn in a food processor to a smooth dough.

To make the tamale dough, beat the lard in a mixer with the salt until light. Add the baking powder and masa dough. Pour in the stock and continue beating for about 5 minutes. Refrigerate for 1 hour. Return the dough to the mixer and beat again for 5 minutes. Stir in the corn kernels and reserve.

To make the filling, melt the butter over medium heat in a large skillet. Add the squash, and sauté for a few minutes, then add the cayenne and season to taste with salt and pepper. Stir in the goat cheese and blossoms.

For the final assembly, place a spoonful of tamale dough inside a corn husk and add a spoonful of the squash mixture. Bundle the mixture inside the husk and secure with a tie made from a strip of husk or with a piece of kitchen string. Repeat until all husks are filled.

Put the tamales in a husk or leaf-lined steam insert, place over a pot of simmering water, and cover. Steam the tamales for about 40 minutes. Check for doneness by opening a bundle: the dough should have a cakelike texture and firm edges.

Variations: Tamales can be filled with virtually anything—leftover chicken or pork, huitlacoche, cooked vegetables or fruit. You can omit the assembly process and instead build a tamale pie. Double the amount of filling, add tomatoes and herbs, then divide the filling among two or three pie pans, spreading the dough evenly on top. Cover each with a large squash leaf and sprinkle each leaf with a tablespoon of water. Put a lid on top of each pan and bake at 350 degrees for 1 hour. The secret to the success of the tamale pie is to be sure there is plenty of liquid in the filling and a little water on the squash leaf to steam the dough.

Grilled Rosa Bianca Eggplant with Roasted Peppers, Cinnamon Basil, and Quark

MAKES 6 SERVINGS

Quark is a German-style cultured milk product similar to yogurt. In this dish it adds a nice tangy balance to the smoke flavors from the grill. If you don't find cinnamon basil, use fresh basil and a grate of cinnamon.

    4 tablespoons (½ stick) unsalted butter

    2 large Rosa Bianca eggplants (or other variety), sliced ¼-inch thick, salted, drained, and patted dry

    Olive oil for brushing

    Salt

    ¼ cup Quark or plain yogurt, stirred until creamy

    Handful cinnamon basil, chopped

    4 fresh Goat Horn peppers or other mild peppers, charred, peeled, seeded, and diced

In a saucepan, melt the butter over medium heat and cook for about 3 to 5 minutes, until the butter solids turn brown and start to smell like toasted hazelnuts. Reserve and keep warm on the back of the stove.

Brush the eggplant with olive oil and season with salt to taste. On the grill, cook the eggplant over medium heat until each side is golden and crisp. Put the eggplant on a platter, drizzle with Quark and the reserved brown butter, then sprinkle with the cinnamon basil and Goat Horn peppers.

Variations: Fresh sweet bell peppers or any hot chiles may be substituted for the Goat Horn peppers. Marjoram, basil, sage, or mint may be substituted for the cinnamon basil.

Spicy Red Haven Peach Sauce
MAKES ABOUT 4 CUPS

This sauce is very popular with visitors at the farm. I usually serve it with roasted pork, but it turns up on pizza, on toast in the morning, and on hamburgers. Use peaches that have blemishes or split pits, and save the perfect ones for eating out of hand.

2 tablespoons olive oil

4 cloves garlic, thinly sliced

1 medium red onion, diced

6 Red Haven peaches, peeled, pitted, and chopped

¾ cup organic sugar (evaporated cane juice)

2 arbol chiles

2 tablespoons chopped fresh rosemary

1 star anise pod, whole

Kosher salt

In a medium saucepan, add the oil, garlic, and onion and heat over medium heat. Sweat the garlic and onion, then add the peaches, sugar, chiles, rosemary, and star anise. Cook gently until thickened. Season to taste with salt. Cool in the pan.

DESSERTS

Peaches with Mascarpone and Nutmeg
MAKES 4 SERVINGS

This simple dessert is designed to show off your best peaches.

¼ cup mascarpone

2 tablespoons organic sugar (evaporated cane juice)

2 ripe peaches, peeled, pitted, and halved

Freshly grated nutmeg

Tree-ripened peaches still warm from the sun. Yum!

In a small bowl, mix by hand the mascarpone and sugar. Put half a peach each in 4 serving bowls and add a dollop of the mascarpone–sugar mixture to each. Sprinkle nutmeg over the top.

Huckleberry Sage Ice Cream

MAKES 1 QUART

Precious huckleberries, foraged in the nearby mountains, make this ice cream very special. Huckleberries are available seasonally at farmers markets, but if you are adventurous enough, you can forage them for yourself. They freeze well for use in pies and sauces.

1 cup huckleberries

2½ cups heavy cream

2 cups goat's milk or cow's milk

8 to 10 sage leaves

8 large egg yolks

¾ cup organic sugar (evaporated cane juice)

¼ teaspoon salt

In a small saucepan, cook the huckleberries over low heat for about 3 minutes, until the skins soften. Reserve.

In another saucepan, heat to scalding the heavy cream, goat's milk, and sage leaves. Turn off the heat and let steep for 10 minutes. Strain out and discard the sage leaves.

Whisk together the egg yolks, sugar, and salt until frothy. Slowly add the cream mixture to the egg–sugar mixture, whisking constantly. Pour this back into the pan and cook over medium-low heat, stirring constantly until the mixture

Huckleberries are foraged a short drive from the farm, up on Monumental Mountain. The queen of wild berries, they taste wonderful in ice cream.

coats the back of a spoon. Stir in the reserved huckleberries. Chill thoroughly. Freeze custard in an ice cream maker according to manufacturer's directions. Transfer ice cream to a covered container and freeze until ready to serve.

Variations: This is a good basic ice cream recipe, with the goat's milk adding a nice tang. You can add almost any herb or fruit. Substitute peaches and apricots for the huckleberries, or make sage ice cream and serve the huckleberries as a sauce.

Summer Harvest List

Apricots	Herbs
Cheese	Huckleberries
Cherries	Lamb
Cherry tomatoes	Leeks
Chicken, duck, and	Lettuces
quail eggs	Mâche
Early corn	Mullein (a medicinal
Early eggplant	herb)
Early plums	Nectarines
Early tomatoes	Peaches
Fava beans	Peppers
Goat	Purslane
Goat's milk	Serviceberries (also
Green beans	called Saskatoons or
Ground cherries (in	juneberries)
the tomatillo family,	Strawberries
they look like tiny	Summer squash
tomatillos and taste	Tomatillos
very sweet)	Watercress
Haricots verts	Zucchini blossoms

SUMMER PANTRY

Alpine Strawberry–Coriander Vinegar
MAKES 2 CUPS (1 PINT JAR)

Use this vinegar for light green salads, dress beets or carrots with it, or add it to fruit salads.

2 cups white wine vinegar
½ cup fresh alpine strawberries or other strawberries
2 tablespoons cracked coriander seed

Pour the white wine vinegar into a large jar, then add the strawberries and coriander seed. Cap tightly and let sit in a cool, dark place for 2 weeks. Strain the vinegar and decant into a pint jar or other vessel. Discard the strawberries and coriander. Store in a cool, dark pantry for up to 6 months.

Borage-Blossom Butter
MAKES 1 POUND

This compound butter can be served with bread on the table or melted and tossed with pasta, blanched beans, or potatoes. The borage blossoms have a cucumber flavor note and a bright blue to soft purple color.

2 cups (4 sticks) unsalted butter, softened
1 cup borage flowers
Pinch of salt

In a food processor, blend the butter, borage flowers, and salt until smooth. Roll the butter in parchment paper and refrigerate. Slice for service, or place in dishes or small serving crocks.

Variations: Any herb or edible flower can be substituted for borage in this butter. Herbs can be chopped and stirred into the butter or puréed with the butter for different color effects.

Tomatillo Salsa
MAKES 4 CUPS

Serve this salsa with tamales, with black beans, or on eggs; or cook with potatoes for *papas verdes.*

1 pound tomatillos, husks removed
1 medium yellow or white onion, chopped coarsely
3 cloves garlic, whole
2 fresh serrano chiles, whole

Eating tomatoes fresh from the vine while harvesting in the garden; that's what it's all about!

2 tablespoons olive oil

1 tablespoon kosher salt

2 tablespoons white wine vinegar

Preheat the oven to 400 degrees F.

In a small mixing bowl, toss the tomatillos, onion, garlic, and chiles with the olive oil and salt. Spread the mixture on a baking tray and roast for about 20 minutes, or until the skins of the tomatillos start to split.

Cool the mixture slightly, then purée in a blender. Add the white wine vinegar and season to taste with salt. Put in a sterilized jar and refrigerate, or process in a hot water bath (for 20 minutes) for the pantry.

Apricot Preserves
MAKES 8 CUPS (4 PINT JARS)

A must for the pantry—and the essential ingredient for our Apricot–Grilled Cheese Breakfast Sandwiches.

6 pounds pitted apricots

6 cups organic sugar (evaporated cane juice)

Mix the apricots and sugar together and let sit in the refrigerator over night. The next day, stir and mash the mixture. Pour in a heavy-bottomed pot and heat over medium, stirring occasionally until the mixture is thick and syrupy. Transfer to sterilized jars. Refrigerate or process in a hot water bath for the pantry.

Dilly Beans with Garlic and Peppercorns
MAKES 6 PINT JARS

An abundance of Provider beans inspired this recipe. Any green bean or wax bean will do nicely. You can play with the spices or herbs in this recipe; just be sure to keep the vinegar-to-water ratio the same.

6 cloves garlic, thinly sliced

30 whole black peppercorns

6 sprigs fresh dill

6 fresh arbol chiles, whole

About 3 pounds tender young green beans, trimmed

3½ cups white wine vinegar

3½ cups water

2 tablespoons pickling salt

Divide the garlic, peppercorns, dill, chiles, and green beans among 6 sterilized pint jars. In a saucepan, combine the white wine vinegar, water, and pickling salt and heat to boiling. Pour the hot vinegar mixture over the beans and cap jars with sterilized lids. Either cool and refrigerate, or process in a hot water bath. Wait 2 weeks before opening. Dilly beans will keep up to 3 months in the refrigerator.

Shopping at local farmstores and establishing relationships with local farmers can answer questions about safe practices and help support a prosperous farming community.

FALL
PRESERVATION

FALL
PRESERVATION

ALTHOUGH SUMMER HAS QUILLISASCUT FARM buzzing like a hive, there is a palpable sense of slowing down as the days get cooler. Thoughts turn to preserving the abundance of summer to keep a bit of its brightness and sustenance for the long winter months. The last few sessions of the year for students are a flurry of canning tomatoes and preserves, drying corn and beans, gathering squash and laying them aside in the cool back room—and, of course, enjoying the ripeness of the foods of fall.

A RESTAURANT COMES TO THE FARM
In mid-September the bunkhouse is transformed: The whole staff of Stumbling Goat Bistro in Seattle's Phinney Ridge neighborhood has arrived for a special session, to learn the life of the farm. Chef Seth Caswell has been looking forward to bringing his staff here for the past year. "We saw a video of the farm at a Chefs Collaborative cheese tasting in Seattle, and I was trying to figure out how we could all have this great experience, and it dawned on me— why don't we just all go?" So he closed the restaurant and packed up his sous-chefs, line cooks, servers, and bartenders, as well as the restaurant's owner, Erin Fettridge, and headed east.

Caswell is no stranger to some of the lessons taught at the farm. He's broken down plenty of whole animals in his day. "When we get a whole animal into the kitchen [at the restaurant], it is my project, and now [here at Quillisascut], I'm excited to step back from it, and see other people experience it for the first time. The kitchen staff is super excited about it." He's right. When the staff arrives—a selection of super-cool twentysomethings with shaggy hair and faded jeans—you wouldn't think they'd be into farming. But as they sit around the long wooden table overflowing with tastes of early autumn's harvest—including a selection of six or seven Quillisascut cheeses, from fresh chèvre to hard-cured curado, as well as cured duck breast, Elstar and Honeycrisp apples, Aunt Molly's ground cherries ("Godiva style," meaning naked), and little green Himrod seedless grapes—they eat together and enthusiastically share their goals.

Bartender Mike McGraw, a lanky, ponytailed hipster who grew up in Argentina, says he would like to "smell the smells, see the sights" of the farm. His brother, Stumbling Goat manager and server Paul McGraw, says, "We had a farm growing up, and we had this terrible donkey that never liked me." The group laughs, especially Rick and Lora Lea, who have had their fair share of stubborn goats. "And I want to learn to make cheese," says Paul. That strikes a chord. Everyone nods, and around the table the new students express their excitement at the chance to experience something new, to make the foods they love to eat.

Fettridge agrees: "I have some farm experience, but I want to see the whole process from beginning to end. In the restaurant we are knowledgeable about what we serve, but this is a fabulous way to get people excited about food and what is good, healthy, and sustainable." She doesn't say much after that except, "I'm in heaven. This cheese is so good!"

RENEWING AMERICA'S FOOD TRADITIONS

As the organic and local food movement gained steam in the 1990s, more and more people began realizing what was being lost through industrial farming. Because these methods focused on producing large quantities of easily packable and transportable fruits and vegetables, the industrial farms were using fewer and fewer varieties of plants. The result was that historical varieties were no longer being planted and exchanged. In *The Revolution Will Not Be Microwaved,* Sandor Ellix Katz describes this loss: "Over the past 100 years, 250,000 plant varieties have gone extinct . . . and the United States has lost 93 percent of its crop diversity."

To stanch the flow of indigenous food items into extinction, and to celebrate and encourage the use of these plants and animals, the international food movement known as Slow Food (see "Rethinking the Kitchen") created a project in 2004 called Renewing America's Food Traditions, or RAFT. RAFT is a coalition of seven ecological organizations—the American Livestock Breeds Conservancy, the Center for Sustainable Environments at Northern Arizona University, Chefs Collaborative, the Cultural Conservancy, Native Seed/SEARCH, Seed Savers Exchange, and Slow Food USA—that have joined forces to document at-risk traditional foods, educate the public about these foods, and promote their reintroduction into food systems across the country. The RAFT mission states that "there is an urgent need to maintain the incredible diversity of America's edible plants, animals, and their food traditions because of the important ecological, gastronomical, cultural, and health benefits of biodiversity."

In its first publication, *Renewing America's Food Traditions,* RAFT identified twelve hundred at-risk fruits, vegetables, and livestock breeds, led by a top-ten list that included Iroquois corn, the American Heritage turkey, and the eulachon (or Columbia River smelt)—a small oily fish important to the culture and diets of Native people, the population of which has declined dramatically in recent years. A forthcoming expanded version of this book promises to be the "most

Rick harvests Galeux d'Eysines winter squash just ahead of the first frost.

ambitious food project in American history, the first book to comprehensively address the current state of culinary treasures unique to the North American continent."

But it's one thing to document these foods and another altogether to see to their increased use and economic viability. One RAFT partner, Seed Savers Exchange, experimented with gathering the seeds of more than twenty endangered foods from the RAFT at-risk list and sending them, free of charge, to farmers and gardeners across the country (including the Misterlys at Quillisascut Farm). These farmers agree to propagate the plants, save the seeds, give feedback to RAFT about the success or nonsuccess of these heritage plants in their own locales, and share the bounties of their labors with others.

PLENTY OF PLEASURE: ENJOYING THE HARVEST

The best part about being on the farm is eating, especially in fall, when so many foods are at their peak and the season seems to invite slowing down. In 2007 a very special dinner took place, not at the farm (although this is always special, too) but at Seattle's Discovery Park, when dozens of food lovers, chefs (many of whom were former students at Quillisascut), and members of Slow Food Seattle and Chefs Collaborative Seattle came together for an historic gathering. This picnic was one of five held across the country (others took place in Shelburne, Vermont; Madison, Wisconsin; Siler City, North Carolina; and Austin, Texas) to celebrate endangered local foods in each region. The Northwest has been designated "Salmon Nation," and the Sunday picnic at Discovery Park featured foods that are found pretty much exclusively in the Northwest.

On the menu was marbled Chinook salmon (a natural genetic mutation that makes a salmon part white and part red inside). This fatty, succulent fish was brought down and barbecued up by Riley Starks and Craig Miller, reefnet fishermen on Lummi Island in Puget Sound's San Juan Islands. Several local chefs cooked up other local delicacies that they

feature on their menus with the goal of revitalizing these historical foods in the local economy. Chef Caswell and his crew from Stumbling Goat brought "Speckled Like a Trout" lettuce with foraged lobster mushrooms and Estrella Family Creamery's Alderwood Smoked Cheese. Chef Tamara Murphy of Seattle's Brasa restaurant brought Ozette potato salad; this potato is one of the few that came to North America not through Europe but straight up the coast from Peru, brought by Spanish explorers in the 1700s. Chef Fernando Divina of

Harvesting dried beans on a lazy afternoon

Farm Profile: Cliffside Orchards
Jeff and Jeanette Herman, Rice, Washington

Jeff Herman drives up in his tractor full of boxes of just-harvested nectarines. He parks and steps out into the shade of his fruit barn, and his wife, Jeanette, hands me one of the gorgeously mottled yellow fruits. "That's a Red Gold," she says. She's been listing off the varieties of apples grown in their organic orchards. "Macintosh, Gala, Empire, Cameo, Winesap, Gravenstein . . ." Jeff interjects, "Honeycrisp. Did you say Cox's Orange Pippin?" "Yes," Jeanette says, "and Spitzenberg, Melrose, Pink Pearl, and Keepsake. They stay crisp for months, and that's what people are looking for."

The Hermans' forty-acre certified organic farm—about two miles from Quillisascut—is a model for organic farming, according to Rick Misterly. "They took a raw piece of land and turned it into an organic orchard. Over the past twenty-five years, they've been through all different forms of selling—wholesale, retail—and when organic produce became more popular and the big guys started doing organic, they adapted to the changing market, growing different varieties to cover the season better." Now the Hermans sell mostly at farmers markets—everything from cherries to eight or so varieties of peaches, three varieties of pears, and eighteen varieties of apples.

"It is amazing how hungry people are for fresh fruit with incredible flavor," says Jeanette. She sells fruit at the University District Farmers Market in Seattle, where the Hermans are constantly educating people about their fruit. "People think you can't get a good ripe peach after August, but we have some varieties of peaches that we harvest later than most people, and some that look green and are actually ripe," she says. She loves the antique and heirloom varieties for their flavor and beauty. "We love what Quillisascut is doing," she says. She sells fruit to several chefs who have been students at Quillisascut, including Darin Leonardson of Google and Craig Hetherington, executive chef at Seattle Art Museum's Taste restaurant. "More chefs and, as a result, more home cooks are learning about what we do, and are making that connection between the farm and the kitchen."

Tendrils Restaurant at SageCliffe, a resort on the banks of the Columbia Gorge in eastern Washington, brought a salad of Pacific chanterelle mushrooms, as well as fresh, pillowy sheep's milk cheese with huckleberries and sage honey. The incredible display of local bounty included one or two dishes that used Quillisascut cheese and the local Inchelium garlic, a variety discovered on a homestead at Inchelium, just miles from Quillisascut. The crowd, of course, ate it up, under surprisingly sunny autumn skies, and everyone wanted to know more about the foods they were eating.

The 180 endangered Northwest foods on the RAFT list are catalogued in the publication *Renewing Salmon Nation's Food Traditions*, a fascinating collection of information on everything from Inchelium garlic to eulachon (also known as ooligan and candlefish). In RAFT jargon each food "nation" has a totem food that represents its primary traditional foods. In addition to Salmon Nation, the others are Chile Pepper Nation, Bison Nation, Pinyon Nut Nation, Moose Nation, Clambake Nation, Wild Rice Nation, Maple Syrup Nation, Crabcake Nation, Gumbo Nation, Cornbread and BBQ

Chef Profile: Peter Hoffman
Savoy Restaurant, New York, New York

Peter Hoffman, chef-owner of Savoy Restaurant in the heart of New York City's Soho district, champions using the freshest produce from local farmers in his very urban kitchen. He's been seen riding his bicycle with a side of beef or an heirloom pig strapped to his back, on his way to a local butcher in Chinatown to have it broken down, or hauling in his large basket trailer a load of produce bought from New York farmers at a local Greenmarket, about a mile away.

After seventeen years at Savoy, Hoffman opened a second restaurant in the East Village, a more casual place called Back 40. "We wanted to see if we could take what we've learned from Savoy and apply that experience in a more informal setting." The restaurant's menu, like Savoy's, focuses on what's in season, which can create problems when a patron wants a tomato in February. But Hoffman is in the business of educating the eater—he's served on the board of the New York Greenmarket Association and as the executive director of Chefs Collaborative, a national nonprofit focused on promoting sustainable practices in the professional kitchen. At Savoy he offers diners the best of what each season has to offer. *The Slow Food Guide to New York* has called the restaurant "as close as it gets to Chez Panisse in New York."

In the fall at Savoy, for instance, Hoffman offers seasonal delicacies such as a whole menu of autumn mushrooms, starting with a matsutake mushroom consommé, a black trumpet mushroom risotto, and a glorious mound of chanterelles atop a grilled venison loin. "We try to get our products as local as possible, but we also source great items from other places around the country." That may mean, for example, introducing restaurant patrons to incredible matsutake and black trumpet mushrooms from the West Coast. For Hoffman, sourcing is about finding the best ingredients and building relationships with foragers, farmers, and ranchers. "In some ways, that is why we decided to call this new restaurant Back 40," he says. "It reminds people that food comes from the agricultural landscape."

Nation, and Chestnut Nation.

Special guest and keynote speaker Gary Paul Nabhan, executive director of the RAFT project, told of his experiences raising Churro sheep—a livestock animal from the Chile Pepper Nation—in Arizona. He voiced his hope that in the following year there would be 150 picnics across the country, and 500 the year after that, eventually culminating in a new national holiday that would celebrate our traditional foods and the farmers, ranchers, fishers, and other producers who are helping to revitalize the food system. Nabhan read his "Terroir-ist's Manifesto for Eating in Place" (a portion of which is excerpted here), a poem that seemed to capture the essence of the day. The poem also reflected the essence of the gathering that night at Discovery Park as a representation of all harvest dinners, whether they be around the teaching table at Quillisascut or in dining rooms throughout the city:

Nothing says fall like fresh pressed apple cider, strained and poured into jugs for the days ahead.

Know where your food has come from
by the very way it tastes:
its freshness telling you
how far it may have traveled,
the hint of mint in the cheese
suggesting what the goat has eaten,
the terroir of the wine
reminding you of the lime
in the stone you stand upon,

so that you can stand up for the land
that has offered it to you.
Know where your food comes from
by the richness of stories told around the table
recalling all that was harvested nearby
during the years that came before you,
when your predecessors & ancestors
roamed the same woods & neighborhoods
where you & yours now roam.

Establishing a Sustainable Focus: A Personal and Professional Perspective
by Chef-Instructor Diana Dillard, Seattle Culinary Academy at Seattle Central Community College

Utter disbelief followed my doctor's diagnosis: the "C" word. Then I went into fight mode and charged into battle as fast and furiously as I could, with four surgeries and six months of chemotherapy. Now, looking back four years later, the only thing that makes any sense to me as to why I got cancer is that it had something to do with the environment and/or with my diet as a child. God bless my dear mother, who did her best but served us Hamburger Helper and, for a special treat, some fluffy white goo out of a jar whose label made a reference to marshmallows.

After the diagnosis, I vowed to purify my body through diet as well as through eliminating my use of harmful chemicals. Concurrently, as fate would have it, the Seattle Culinary Academy (SCA), where at the time I had worked for fifteen years, was determined to establish a sustainable focus to its curriculum. I was by no means the driving force behind this mission. A part of it, yes, and an avid supporter by all means, but it took the passion and dedication of the entire team to make it happen. Serendipitously, my personal and professional life merged in a profound way.

The SCA and the Quillisascut Farm School, through shared and aligned passion, began a scholarship program for culinary students and faculty to attend farm sessions. How could I possibly teach something without having experienced it firsthand? I attended a professional retreat at the farm three months after the end of my treatment. I walked away from the retreat renewed, reenergized, and with a wealth of knowledge to take back to my students and to live by personally. At the SCA we now order product strictly by the season, we have become compost Nazis, and we don't leave water running unless it's absolutely necessary. These examples have become habits, and we no longer have to think consciously about them. We use eco-friendly cleaning supplies, and a plan is in place to build a sustainable greenhouse, where we will use organic methods to grow many of the herbs, fruits, and vegetables we use in the campus restaurants.

Quinces smell divine but need to be cooked and sweet-
ened before eating; they are full of pectin, which thickens
jam and other sweet treats.

Farm Profile: Riverview Orchard and Crandall Coffee Roasters
John and Janet Crandall, Kettle Falls, Washington

Resting on a bluff overlooking Lake Roosevelt, John and Janet Crandall's ten-acre Riverview Orchard in Kettle Falls, Washington, grows certified organic fruits, including cherries, nectarines, peaches, plums, pears, apples, and raspberries. Students and chefs who study at Quillisascut usually go on a day trip to Riverview to get a sense of the farm community that Quillisascut is a part of and to experience some of the area's history—not to mention to graze at the trees and the berry patches for some of the sweetest, most succulent fruit available anywhere.

In this orchard several nearly sixty-five-year-old Bing cherry trees stand as a reminder of the orchard planted by the original owners, who had to move their operation from the lower banks of the Columbia River before Grand Coulee Dam was completed in 1940. The orchard has seen four owners since that time. It has undergone much planting and many changes in operation and merchandising, as have all the farms in the Lake Roosevelt area. The Crandalls sell their fruit wholesale, fresh at their farm's fruit stand, and at various farmers markets. Nonmarketable fruit is made into jam or dried, and the apples are pressed into apple cider.

But even so, the Crandalls must supplement that seasonal income, as most farmers must do. They have discovered coffee roasting. It has become not only an important part of their livelihood but a passion—and one that the local community shares. The Crandalls roast their coffee in the morning and ship it that same afternoon. Often the freshly roasted coffee is held in the local post office overnight, so the delicious aroma is the first thing the postal workers encounter in the morning. Needless to say, they love to brew up a pot of Crandall's each morning.

BACK IN THE CITY: APPLYING LESSONS FROM THE FARM AT HOME

If you read through the farm's notebook, a sort of yearbook that all the students sign, so many of the comments are similar to those of Anita Chhun, who wrote, "This was the best week of my life." She expressed a common sentiment among departing students: "Before I came here, my first instinct would have been to go buy what I needed and I never thought about all the hands that have touched it to make it possible. But now I just want to make everything myself, or get it from an artisan. There's more I want to say, but can't put it into words." Chhun continued: "My soul feels better and I have hope for the future."

That's what this farm is all about: hope for the future. Each winter, the farmers dream of what is possible, and each spring, as seeds are planted and kids are born, those possibilities seem real. But it isn't until the hands of these new farmers, gardeners, and chefs bring their creativity, nurturing, community, and care to the process, that the vision of the Quillisascut Farm School really works. This microcosm of the community—the town and city, the country and the world—can be observed and learned from: the cycles of seasons, the observance of nature's message, and the transformation of our dreams into work toward more sustainable communities with a deeper connection to our food and to ourselves.

Goats head towards the barn at the end of the day.

FALL
RECIPES

THE HARVEST RUSH BEFORE THE FROST requires that we bring the storage crops into the cellar. Kitchen work includes braiding onions and garlic, hanging corn to dry. There are also pressing cider, drying plums, roasting chiles, and making tomato paste. Butchering ducks, shelling beans, and making sauerkraut keeps us busy, too. We warm ourselves with hearty soups and braises. The culmination of the harvest season is the making of the cassoulet . . . all of our work from the summer is reflected in this dish.

Lavosh with goat cheese and Crab Apple–Rose Hip Geleé

BREAKFAST & BREADS

Lavosh

MAKES 8 LARGE CRACKERS, APPROXIMATELY 9 BY 14 INCHES

These crisp flatbread crackers hail from Armenia. They are a dramatic complement to the farm's cheese displays. We brush them with olive oil and coarse sea salt and top with different herbs (rosemary and thyme) or seed spices (nigella, caraway, cumin, or poppy) for color and flavor variation.

    3 tablespoons active dry yeast (4 packets)
    3 cups warm water
    2 cups whole wheat flour
    5 cups all-purpose or bread flour
    ¼ cup finely chopped fresh herbs (rosemary, mint,
        sage, or your choice)
    1 tablespoon kosher salt

Mix the yeast with the water and let sit in a warm place until it foams. Put the water–yeast mixture in a large mixing bowl and stir in the whole wheat and white flours, herbs, and salt. Add more flour if the dough is too sticky. Let rise until doubled in bulk, then punch down with your fist to deflate the risen yeast dough.

Preheat the oven to 350 degrees F.

Roll the dough very thinly and evenly, large enough to cover a baking sheet. You should make about 8 large sheets of dough. Place the dough sheets on ungreased baking sheets and bake in batches for about 15 minutes, or until crisp and golden, flipping once.

Serve crackers whole for dramatic presentation, or break up into pieces if desired. Only garnish the crackers that you are serving immediately; the dry crackers will keep well stored in an airtight container for a week or more.

SOUPS & SALADS

Vanilla–Pear Vinaigrette
MAKES 1 CUP

This vinaigrette is excellent for a contrast to the sturdier, slightly bitter greens that flourish in the fall, such as arugula, mizuna, and kale.

¼ cup apple cider
¼ cup pear nectar
¼ vanilla bean, split
½ cassia stick or cinnamon stick
¼ cup white balsamic vinegar
½ cup canola oil
Salt and pepper

In a small saucepot over low heat, simmer the apple cider, pear nectar, vanilla bean, and cassia stick. Reduce to ¼ cup. Remove and discard the vanilla bean and cassia stick. Transfer the mixture to a blender and add the white balsamic vinegar, canola oil, and salt and pepper to taste. Blend thoroughly and use within a few days.

Doukhobor Borscht
MAKES ABOUT 1 GALLON (16 CUPS)

The Doukhobors were pacifists exiled from Russia at the end of the nineteenth century (around 1897). They settled just across the U.S. border in Canada. This recipe for borscht is based on my childhood memories of eating at the Yale Hotel in Grand Forks, British Columbia. It is not primarily a beet-based soup. This soup is often served with a pat of butter on

A local farmer, Dick Roberson, relaxes after getting his garlic harvest into storage.

the top; sometimes it's spooned on top of bread; or bread and butter can be dunked into the soup. It's better the next day, and it also freezes well.

6 medium potatoes (about 2 pounds), peeled, quartered, plus 1 potato diced
5 large yellow onions, diced and divided
1 large red beet, peeled and left whole
4 tablespoons kosher salt
4 ears sweet corn, kernels removed (cobs and kernels reserved)
¾ cup heavy cream, divided

1 cup (2 sticks) unsalted butter, divided

4 cloves garlic, finely chopped

1 cup tomato sauce

4 beefsteak tomatoes, seeded and chopped, reserving the juice

1 small head green cabbage, finely chopped, reserving 2 cups

2 large green peppers, seeded and diced

½ cup shredded carrot

½ cup chopped fresh dill

1 tablespoon smoked paprika (store-bought, also called Spanish paprika)

¼ cup cider vinegar

Freshly ground black pepper

In a large stockpot, bring to a boil 3 quarts of water, the potatoes, 1 cup of the onions, beet, and salt. Put the corncobs in the stockpot.

After a fall rain, Shaggy Mane mushrooms are foraged from between the raised beds in the schoolyard.

In a food processor, roughly chop the corn kernels and blend with half of the heavy cream. Season to taste with salt and pepper. Reserve. When the potatoes are soft, remove from the water and mash with 1 stick of the butter and the remaining heavy cream. Add the corn kernel–cream mixture, season with salt, and reserve. Remove the cobs and beet from the stockpot and discard.

Melt 2 tablespoons of the butter in a large saucepan over medium heat. Cook the remaining onions and the garlic until soft, about 7 minutes. Add the tomato sauce, beefsteak tomatoes, and reserved juice. Cook until thick and saucy, and season to taste with salt and pepper. Add the tomato mixture to the stockpot.

In another saucepan, cook the cabbage (except for the reserved 2 cups) in 4 tablespoons of the butter until soft. Add to the stockpot. Now add the reserved mashed potato–corn mixture to the stockpot. Stir briefly and let cook for 5 minutes.

Add to the stockpot the diced potato, remaining raw cabbage, green peppers, carrot, dill, paprika, and remaining butter. Cook until the potatoes are soft, about 15 minutes. Stir in the cider vinegar, black pepper, and salt to taste. Adjust the amount of paprika if desired. Serve with hearty wheat bread and butter.

Cured Beef Tongue with Chervil and Sweet Onion Salad

MAKES 4 SERVINGS

This simple salad is tasty as a side dish or served on top of a slice of hearty rye bread. Serve it for breakfast with hard-cooked eggs and slices of cheese. Beef tongue is readily available from your local butcher. To cure the tongue yourself, see the Cured Beef Tongue recipe in the "Fall Pantry" section of this chapter. Cured tongue is also available in most delis and specialty stores.

Cured Beef Tongue with Chervil and Sweet Onion Salad

Freshly made lamb sausage

1 cup raisins

¼ cup cherry vinegar or other fruit-flavored vinegar

1 small sweet onion, sliced into thin rings

12 ounces cured beef tongue, sliced very thin

¼ cup fresh whole chervil leaves

¼ teaspoon toasted and ground coriander

4 tablespoons extra virgin olive oil

Salt and pepper

In a medium bowl, soak the raisins in the cherry vinegar and reserve. In another bowl, cover the onion with cold water and soak for 20 minutes before draining well. Toss together the reserved raisin–cherry vinegar mixture, onion, beef tongue, chervil, coriander, and olive oil. Season to taste with salt and pepper. Let stand for 10 minutes before serving.

Ceci Bean, Kielbasa, and Sauerkraut Soup

MAKES 1 GALLON (16 CUPS)

Ceci beans, also known as chickpeas or garbanzo beans, are successfully grown in the Northwest and therefore a staple in the Quillisascut kitchen. Depending on variety, color ranges from pale yellow to inky black. Soak the beans the night before you want to use them for faster cooking the next day.

6 cups ceci beans, soaked overnight in 12 cups water
     (reserve soaking water)

4 tablespoons kosher salt

2 large yellow onions, cut into thin strips from base to top

8 to 10 cloves garlic, finely chopped

2 fresh or dried bay leaves

6 whole black peppercorns

2 tablespoons chopped fresh dill

1½ tablespoons coriander seed, toasted and ground

2 pounds freshly ground kielbasa or other mild sausage

2 cups naturally fermented sauerkraut, room temperature (see the Sauerkraut recipe later in this chapter)

Pour the beans and soaking water into a large stockpot and bring to a simmer over low heat. Skim any foam from the top. Add the salt and continue cooking for 20 minutes. Add the onions, garlic, bay leaves, and peppercorns, and simmer uncovered until the beans are soft and buttery in flavor. Add the dill and coriander and cook for 10 minutes more.

Meanwhile, on a cutting board roll the kielbasa into 2-ounce balls. In a large skillet, brown the kielbasa meatballs on all sides, then cover and continue cooking until juices run clear. Keep warm, covered, until ready to serve.

To serve, ladle the soup into bowls, top each with 2 tablespoons of sauerkraut and a kielbasa meatball. Garnish with chopped fresh chives if desired. Serve immediately.

Variations: Top the soup with fresh cabbage, onions, and chorizo sausage. Season the soup with cumin and chiles. For an Adriatic meal, top with lamb sausage, cucumbers, fresh mint, and plain yogurt. The sauerkraut balances the richness of the ceci beans in this soup. If you want to omit the sauerkraut, adjust the acid by adding ½ cup vinegar.

Ceci Bean, Kielbasa, and Sauerkraut Soup

Ozette Fingerling and Lazy Housewife Bean Salad
MAKES 6 SERVINGS

Ozette fingerling potatoes are one of only two potatoes that were directly brought north to the United States from Peru. Most other potatoes went to Europe first and were brought west by immigrants. The Ozette came to Washington and was planted at a Spanish fort near Neah Bay. The Spaniards left and the Natives nurtured the potatoes for generations. The Ozette has been recognized by Slow Food's Ark of Taste. Lazy Housewife beans are RAFT listed.

Lemon verbena vinaigrette:
- ¼ cup lemon verbena leaves
- 1 tablespoon organic sugar (evaporated cane juice)
- ½ cup white wine vinegar
- 1¼ cups organic canola oil
- Salt and pepper

Salad:
- 1 cup finely diced cucumbers
- 2½ cups (about 8 ounces) Lazy Housewife beans or other green beans, trimmed and cut on the diagonal into ¼-inch slices
- 6 Ozette fingerling potatoes (about ½ pound), sliced in ¼-inch rings
- ¼ cup borage flowers
- Sea salt

To prepare the vinaigrette, bash up the verbena leaves with the sugar in a mortar until bruised. Add the white wine vinegar to the mortar and let steep for 15 minutes. Put the mixture and the canola oil into a blender and purée until emulsified. Strain and season to taste with salt.

To prepare the salad, pour a quarter of the vinaigrette over the cucumbers and reserve. Blanch the beans in a pot of salted water for 2 to 3 minutes, until bright green. Remove the beans (reserve the water) and shock in cold water to stop cooking. Next, boil the potatoes in the salted water for 5 to 7 minutes, until fork-tender but still intact. Shock in cold water.

To serve, arrange the potato slices on plates and scatter with beans. Top with the reserved cucumbers and drizzle with the remaining vinaigrette and high-quality extra virgin olive oil. Sprinkle with the borage flowers and sea salt.

Variations: A creamy cucumber or walnut vinaigrette would also be nice with this salad.

ENTRÉES

Ricotta Gnocchi with Sibley Squash, Pears, and Sage
MAKES 6 TO 8 SERVINGS

Quillisascut Farm has an abundance of fresh ricotta, therefore we love to use this gnocchi recipe, varying the sauces through the seasons. The gnocchi are lighter in texture than traditional potato gnocchi.

Gnocchi:
- 4 cups (about 2 pounds) ricotta cheese
- 1 large egg
- 2 cups all-purpose flour
- 4 tablespoons chopped fresh sage
- 1 tablespoon freshly grated nutmeg
- Kosher salt
- Freshly ground black pepper
- Olive oil for coating

Ricotta Gnocchi with Sibley Squash, Pears, and Sage

Sauce:

>About 2 pounds Sibley squash or other hard
>>squash variety, seeded and halved
>
>Freshly grated nutmeg
>
>Kosher salt
>
>Freshly ground black pepper
>
>1 cup (2 sticks) unsalted butter
>
>6 to 8 sage leaves
>
>3 ripe pears, cored and sliced

>¼ cup freshly grated Parmesan

To prepare the gnocchi:

Bring a large pot of salted water to a boil. In a large bowl, combine the ricotta cheese, egg, flour, sage, nutmeg, salt, and pepper with a wooden spoon until the dough is a workable, firm but soft consistency. Pinch off a teaspoon-size bit of dough for a test: Put this bit of dough into the pot of boiling water, and cook until it floats. Remove, cool slightly, then taste and adjust seasonings if necessary.

Divide the prepared dough into a dozen pieces. Using your palms, roll pieces of dough into long cylinders on a work table lightly sprinkled with flour until they are about ½ inch in diameter. Cut the cylinders into ½-inch sections and roll each section into a ball. Press and flatten the dough ball onto the back of a fork and roll the outer edge toward you as you pinch together lightly, creating a ruffled edge on one side of the gnocchi and a divot to catch sauce. Repeat this process until the dough is gone. Place gnocchi on a flour-dusted baking sheet until ready to cook. (At this point, the gnocchi can be frozen for use another time.)

In small batches, boil until tender, about 3 minutes (they will float to the top). Let float 1 minute more, then remove with a slotted spoon. Toss the gnocchi with a little bit of olive oil and reserve or store in the refrigerator until ready to use.

To prepare the sauce:

Preheat the oven to 400 degrees F.

Place the squash facedown on a greased baking sheet and bake until flesh is soft, about 15 minutes. Turn off the oven. Scoop the flesh from the squash, mash, and season to taste with nutmeg, salt, and pepper. Keep warm in the cooling oven.

Melt the butter over medium heat in a small saucepan. Add the sage leaves and continue cooking until the butter solids turn brown and smell like hazelnuts. Remove from heat, cover, and keep warm.

In a sauté pan, heat 2 tablespoons of the brown butter over medium heat and stir in the pears until they caramelize. Season with salt and pepper, remove from pan, and reserve. In the same pan, heat the reserved brown butter in batches (2 tablespoons at a time) and brown the gnocchi. Season to taste with salt and pepper.

To serve, put a dollop of squash in the middle of each plate, scatter the gnocchi, and top with the reserved caramelized pears. Drizzle with remaining sage butter, and sprinkle with Parmesan.

Variations: Fried sage leaves are a great way to garnish this dish. Simply fry the leaves in a shallow bit of hot oil for about 2 minutes, or until they turn bright green and glassy. Drain well and salt to taste. In springtime, try these gnocchi with spring peas, green onions, and mint.

Huckleberry Cider-Glazed Chicken

MAKES 4 SERVINGS

At the farm we use frozen huckleberries from our summer foraging and fresh apple cider for this dish.

2 cups huckleberries
¼ cup diced shallots
2 cups apple cider
4 cups chicken stock
Kosher salt
Freshly ground black pepper

1 whole chicken, backbone removed and flattened
4 tablespoons chicken fat, lard, or oil

Preheat the oven to 400 degrees F.

To prepare the glaze, purée the huckleberries in a blender and reserve. In a saucepan over medium heat, combine the reserved huckleberries, shallots, apple cider, and chicken stock. Reduce to about 2 cups. Strain, season with salt and pepper, and reserve glaze.

Huckleberry Cider-Glazed Chicken

Rub the chicken with salt, pepper, and fat. Heat in a heavy cast-iron skillet on the stovetop, over high heat for about 3 minutes. Put the chicken in the pan, breast-side down. Place the skillet in the oven and cook for about 20 minutes. Turn the chicken breast-side up and glaze with a bit of the reserved glaze. Cook for another 10 minutes and glaze again. Continue this process until the chicken is done, about 20 minutes more or until the internal temperature reaches 165 degrees F.

Let the chicken rest for 10 minutes before carving. Serve with the glaze pooled over.

Variations: Try grape juice, blackberry juice, pear nectar, or quince nectar in place of the huckleberry cider.

Duck Breast with Chokecherry Sauce

MAKES 4 SERVINGS

Chokecherries—a Northwest native with small, dark-purple stone fruits that are puckery but delicious—grow wild around our farm. They were an important food for the Native peoples and a tasty treat for foragers. Domestic cherries or huckleberries may be substituted in this recipe.

Sauce:

2 to 3 cups duck or chicken stock

2 cups chokecherries

Salt

Freshly ground black pepper

Duck breasts:

2 tablespoons duck fat

4 medium-size duck breasts

Kosher salt

Freshly ground black pepper

Fall Harvest List

Almonds	Peppers
Apples	Pine nuts
Cabbage	Plums
Cheeses	Potatoes
Chokecherries	Quince
Corn	Rose hips
Early winter squash	Roses
Eggplant	Shell beans
Eggs	Tomatoes
Elderberries	Turkey, duck, pork,
Garbanzos	beef, chicken,
Goat's milk	lamb, goat, quail
Grapes	Walnuts
Hazelnuts	Watercress
Herbs	Wild mushrooms:
Kales	shaggy manes,
Lentils	porcini, saffron
Lettuces	milk caps, lepiotas
Pears	

In a large saucepot, bring the stock and chokecherries to a simmer and cook until the chokecherries burst their skins. Put the sauce through a strainer, smashing the chokecherries to remove the juices. Discard the pits. Return the sauce to the saucepot and reduce to 1 cup. Season to taste with salt and pepper. Reserve.

To prepare the duck breast, preheat oven to 400 degrees F.

On the stovetop, melt the duck fat in an ovenproof skillet over high heat. Place the duck breasts skin side down and sear for about 2 to 3 minutes, or until the skin is golden. Turn the breasts and place the skillet in the oven, cooking for about 6 minutes. The duck breasts should be just firm to the touch in the center (medium rare).

Let the breasts rest for 3 to 4 minutes, then slice and fan out on plates. Serve with the reserved chokecherry sauce.

A collection of Quillisascut cheese is traditionally served to students at their first roundtable discussion.

Asador Cumin-Rubbed Gigot of Goat

MAKES 6 SERVINGS

This preparation is delicious made in the farm kitchen's wood-fired oven. We have adapted the recipe here for a standard oven. Goat can be procured at halal Middle Eastern, Italian, and Latino butcher shops, or from your local farmers market. Goat meat is similar to lamb but with a milder flavor.

Brine:

16 cups water

2 tablespoons cumin seed

1½ cups kosher salt

1½ cups organic sugar (evaporated cane juice)

2 chipotle chiles

1 teaspoon whole black peppercorns

1 goat leg, fell removed, boned out (keep bones),
    rolled and tied

Rub:

6 to 8 garlic cloves, thinly sliced

4 tablespoons lard or oil

4 tablespoons whole cumin seed, toasted
    and coarsely ground

4 dried arbol or chipotle chiles, crushed

4 tablespoons kosher salt

To prepare the brine, bring the water, cumin seed, salt, sugar, chiles, and peppercorns to a boil in a large stockpot on the stovetop. Let steep for 15 minutes, then refrigerate. When the brine is cool, place goat leg in brine and refrigerate for at least 4 hours or overnight.

Preheat the oven to 450 degrees F.

Remove the goat leg from the brine and pat dry. Cut small slits in the goat leg and place the garlic inside. Mix together the lard, cumin, chiles, and salt. Rub the goat leg with the mixture. Put the reserved goat bones on a rimmed baking sheet, place the goat leg on top, and roast in oven until medium rare, about 35 to 40 minutes. The internal temperature should be 135 degrees F. Remove from the oven and let rest for 8 to 10 minutes.

While the baking sheet is still hot, pour about ¼ cup of hot water onto baking sheet and scrape up the caramel bits left from the lamb. Pour the drippings into a small saucepot and skim the fat. Simmer, uncovered, for about 3 minutes. Remove from the heat and keep warm on the back of the stove.

Slice the goat leg and serve with the reserved pan drippings.

Variations: Serve with Chimichurri or Tomatillo Salsa (see recipes for each in the "Summer Recipes" chapter).

Rabbit Tart with Pinot Noir–Juniper Sauce

MAKES ONE 9-INCH TART (6 TO 8 SERVINGS)

Featuring tender braised rabbit nestled in a puffed lattice shell with root vegetables and a rich wine sauce, this tart is both comforting and elegant. Use a good quality wine for the juniper sauce and pair the tart with the same wine at the table. Serve a simply dressed salad of spicy fall greens to contrast the richness of the tart. This recipe can easily be adapted to make individual tartlets. Make the puff pastry ahead (recipe follows) or use 2½ pounds frozen puff pastry. Juniper berries are available in the spice section of most supermarkets.

Puff pastry:

2 cups bread flour

½ teaspoons kosher salt

1½ cups (3 sticks) cold unsalted butter, cut into
    1-inch pieces

About ½ cup cold water

Marinade and tart filling:

One 2- to 2½-pound rabbit, whole (remove organ
    meats and reserve for another use)

1 750 ml bottle pinot noir

1 cup chicken stock

Rabbit Tart with Pinot Noir–Juniper Sauce

6 medium yellow onions, julienned (reserve half
    the onions for caramelizing), divided

1 pound carrots, peeled and sliced

½ pound parsnips, peeled and sliced

1 teaspoon whole black peppercorns

5 fresh juniper berries

2 fresh bay leaves

2 tablespoons olive oil

Kosher salt

Cracked black pepper

2 teaspoons chopped fresh thyme leaves

Egg wash:

1 egg

Splash of heavy cream

Juniper sauce:

- 2 cups pinot noir
- Reserved braising liquid from rabbits
- 1 cup chicken stock
- 1 teaspoon dried juniper berries
- 1 cup heavy cream
- Salt

For the puff pastry:

Combine the flour and salt in a stand mixer. Using a dough hook, add the butter to the flour mixture on low. Mix in just enough of the water so that the dough can be handled. Mix for another minute or so, just until the dough comes together. Some lumps of the butter will remain whole.

On a floured board, shape the dough into a rectangle. Roll out to ½-inch thick, keeping the rectangle shape. Fold the edges of the dough to the center, like an envelope. Fold the opposite sides of the dough together like a book. Rotate the dough a quarter turn on the board and roll out into a rectangular shape again. Repeat the entire process one more time, then repeat the envelope and book folds, wrap tightly, and refrigerate for 1 hour. Repeat the roll-and-fold process. Refrigerate until ready to use.

For the marinade and tart filling:

Put the rabbit, pinot noir, stock, half the onions, carrots, parsnips, black peppercorns, juniper berries, and bay leaves into a large braising pan. Cover and marinate in the refrigerator for 4 hours or overnight.

Preheat the oven to 300 degrees F.

Put the braising pan in the oven, covered, and cook for about 3 hours, or until the rabbit meat falls easily from the bone.

Drain the rabbit and vegetables, reserving the liquid. When cool enough to handle, pull the rabbit meat from the bones and shred. Return the meat to the pan and ladle just enough of the braising liquid over it to keep moist. Discard the bones.

Heat the olive oil in a skillet over medium-low heat until it slides easily across the pan. Add the reserved onions. Cover and cook for about 3 minutes, until the onions are soft. Remove the lid and turn up the heat to medium, stirring occasionally, until the onions are brown and sweet. Add the onions to the rabbit–vegetable mixture and season to taste with salt and pepper. Reserve.

For the tart assembly:

Preheat the oven to 400 degrees F.

Roll out two-thirds of the puff pastry ¼-inch thick. Line the bottom and sides of a 9-inch springform pan. Roll out and cut the remaining dough into strips for the lattice crust. Layer into the pastry shell the caramelized onions and the rabbit-vegetable mixture.

Arrange the dough strips in a lattice across the top of the tart. Prepare an egg wash by whisking together the egg and heavy cream. Brush the top of the tart with the egg wash, tuck in the lattice edges along the inside, turn the edges of the tart back and slightly over the lattice to seal, and brush again with the egg wash.

Sprinkle with salt, cracked pepper, and thyme if desired. Put the tart in the oven and bake until the crust is golden, about 35 to 40 minutes. Let rest for 10 minutes, release springform pan, and cut into 6 to 8 portions.

For the juniper sauce:

In a small saucepan, gently heat the pinot noir and flame to burn off the alcohol. In an uncovered 2-quart saucepan over medium heat, bring the reserved braising liquid, chicken stock, juniper berries, and wine to a simmer. Reduce to 2 cups, then strain. Return sauce to pan and add the heavy cream. Continue to reduce until thickened. Season to taste with salt. Set the cover askew and keep warm over low heat until ready to serve with the tart.

Variations: Add sautéed sweetbreads or roasted chestnuts to the filling. Make the tart with chicken instead of rabbit, using white wine in both the marinade and the sauce. For a forager's twist, use wild mushrooms instead of the root vegetables.

Quillisascut Cassoulet
MAKES 8 TO 12 SERVINGS

This dish is special to Quillisascut. We spend the whole summer working toward it—saving bread ends, making sausage and duck confit, butchering lamb and chickens, harvesting and shelling beans. Allow three days to prepare this dish. The first day is for soaking the beans. The second day will entail the bulk of the work, and the third day will require some assembly. Then you can put your feet up and enjoy the long, slow cooking process and delicious smells of the cassoulet. Cassoulet is unique to each region in France. We encourage you to tweak this recipe to reflect your region and culture.

Note: Canned beans are not a suitable substitute as the beans make their own stock and sauce.

Day 1
Beans:

3 pounds flageolet beans, soaked overnight (3 parts water to 1 part beans) in a large stockpot

Lamb shanks braising for Quillisascut Cassoulet, which is assembled from previous projects of harvesting and butchering

Day 2
Pork hock:

1 smoked pork hock or bacon rind

8 to 10 cloves garlic, whole

2 dried bay leaves

2 tablespoons kosher salt

1 teaspoon whole black peppercorns

Lamb shanks:

2 small lamb shanks (about 2 pounds), bone in

1 cup red table wine

2 cloves garlic, whole

4 juniper berries

2 fresh bay leaves

Chicken:

4 chicken thighs (about 1 pound)

1 cup white wine

4 sprigs fresh thyme

1 teaspoon lavender buds

1 fresh bay leaf

Bread crumbs:

½ cup duck fat

3 cups bread crumbs

1 tablespoon chopped fresh thyme

1 tablespoon kosher salt

1 teaspoon freshly ground black pepper

Day 3

Cassoulet:

Reserved beans, lamb shanks, chicken thighs, and bread crumbs from Day 2

Olive oil for browning

1 pound andouille sausage

Kosher salt

Freshly ground black pepper

6 tablespoons duck fat, divided

2 cloves garlic, sliced

3 ripe Roma tomatoes, seeded and coarsely chopped

1 medium yellow onion, diced

2 tablespoons fresh thyme, leaves picked

Freshly grated nutmeg

4 hindquarters duck confit (see Duck Confit in the "Fall Pantry" section)

For day 1:

Soak the beans overnight in a large stockpot.

For day 2:

Drain the beans and cover with water again. Add the pork hock, garlic, bay leaves, salt, and peppercorns. Bring the water up to a simmer slowly. Skim any impurities. Cook for 20 to 40 minutes. When the beans are done, they will have a creamy texture but still be intact. Pour the beans and their liquid into an uncovered container and store overnight in the refrigerator.

Put the lamb, red wine, garlic, juniper berries, and bay leaves in a glass or stainless steel bowl. Cover and refrigerate overnight. In a glass dish or bowl, add the chicken, wine, thyme, lavender buds, and bay leaf. Cover and refrigerate overnight.

Preheat the oven to 350 degrees F.

Melt the duck fat in a small saucepan over low heat. Toss with the bread crumbs, thyme, salt, and pepper in a small bowl. Spread the bread crumbs on a baking sheet and toast in the oven for 8 to 12 minutes, or until golden. Refrigerate overnight.

For day 3:

Preheat the oven to 300 degrees F.

Drain the beans but reserve the liquid and pork hock.

In a heavy-bottomed skillet, heat the olive oil over medium-high until the oil slides easily across the pan. Brown the andouille sausage. Remove from heat, slice, and reserve.

Remove the lamb shanks from the marinade, discard the mari nade, and season the shanks with salt and pepper. In a sauté pan over high heat, add a splash of olive oil and sear the outside of the shanks. Reserve. Remove the reserved chicken thighs from the marinade, discard the marinade, and season the chicken to taste with salt and pepper. In a sauté pan over high heat, add a splash of olive oil and sear the thighs until brown. Reserve.

Melt 4 tablespoons of the duck fat in the bottom of a large, deep roasting pan or cassoulet pan. Remove from the heat and begin layering into the pan, with the beans scattered throughout, the garlic, tomatoes, onion, lamb shanks, pork hock, duck confit, chicken thighs, andouille sausage, thyme, nutmeg, salt, pepper, and finally more beans. Make certain that all of the meats are covered with the beans.

Pour the reserved bean water just above the level of the beans (keep the remaining bean liquid until the cassoulet is done). Dot the top of the cassoulet with the remaining duck fat.

Cover and bake for 1 hour, then uncover and top with the reserved bread crumbs (push them just below the surface of the liquid but do not stir them in). The cassoulet should cook slowly. The fats will rise to the surface and form a crust with the crumbs. Be careful to keep the liquid level above the beans; you may have to add more reserved bean liquid. Every 45 minutes, crack the surface crust, sinking the crumbs under the fat. If the bread crumbs get too brown, cover the pan loosely with foil. The cassoulet should cook for about 4 hours.

Let rest for 20 minutes. Serve warm, with crusty French bread and a hearty red wine.

Michelle Wesley, right, laughs with Chef Kären, center, as they prepare a grape-leaf-wrapped lamb tenderloin dinner for a professional culinary retreat.

DESSERTS

Quince and Goat Cheese Cake
MAKES 8 SERVINGS

Quinces start to ripen in late October, and their smell is heady. We pick a few for the table to freshen the room, a few for lamb tagine (a Morrocan stew), and the bulk for *membrillo* (a Spanish quince paste) and quince jam. This layer cake shows off the pretty amber color of the quince jam and contrasts its sweetness with the tang of chèvre (something that we have in abundance here at Quillisascut). The classic combination of quince and vanilla is, well, simply heaven. Be careful not to overwhip the chèvre or it will become runny.

Cake:
   3 eggs
   1 cup organic sugar (evaporated cane juice)
   ½ cup organic canola oil
   ½ teaspoon pure vanilla extract
   1½ cups all-purpose flour
   1½ teaspoons baking powder
   ½ cup whole milk

Filling:
   2 pounds fresh chèvre
   ¾ cup organic sugar (evaporated cane juice)
   1 jar (16 ounces) quince jam or membrillo (Spanish
      quince paste)
   ¼ cup toasted hazelnuts or pine nuts, coarsely chopped

Preheat the oven to 350 degrees F. Grease and flour two 8-inch round cake pans.

A bowl full of green hued eggs from the farm's
Araucana chickens

Whisk together the eggs and sugar until light and fluffy. Stir in the oil and vanilla. Combine the flour and baking powder. Mix dry ingredients into egg mixture in batches, alternating with milk. Spread the batter evenly into the prepared cake pans. Bake for 30 to 40 minutes, or until a toothpick comes out clean. Remove from the oven and cool in the cake pans on a wire rack.

Remove the cakes from the pans. Slice each layer in half horizontally to get a total of four layers.

To prepare the filling, lightly whip the chèvre with the organic sugar. To assemble, place one layer of cake on a serving plate; spread with the quince jam and then the goat cheese mixture. Repeat with the remaining three cake layers, ending with jam and the cheese mixture.

Sprinkle hazelnuts on top. Chill for 1 hour. Remove from the refrigerator and serve.

Plum Suet Pudding with Hard Sauce
MAKES 8 SERVINGS

This recipe comes from my grandmother, Wilma Jurgensen—grandmother, forager, and culinary inspiration—who combined her mother's plum pudding with her mother-in-law's sauce. The original recipe says to steam the pudding in tin cans, and the sauce is made on the back of a wood-burning stove. Wilma still makes this dish on special occasions. Suet can be purchased from your local butcher.

Pudding:
   2 cups pitted Italian or Green Gage plums, quartered
   1 cup dried bread crumbs
   1 cup all-purpose flour

1 cup organic sugar (evaporated cane juice)

3 teaspoons baking powder

¾ teaspoons kosher salt

½ teaspoon ground cinnamon

¼ teaspoon ground cloves

1 cup whole milk

1 cup ground suet

3 eggs, well beaten

Sauce:

4 tablespoons (½ stick) unsalted butter

1 cup whole milk, plus a splash of milk

1½ cups organic sugar (evaporated cane juice), divided

1 egg

1 tablespoon all-purpose flour

For the pudding:

In a small saucepan over medium heat, cook the plums with ¼ cup water until liquefied. Cook for another 8 to 10 minutes, until slightly thickened. Reserve.

In a mixing bowl, sift the bread crumbs, flour, sugar, baking powder, and salt with the cinnamon and cloves. In a separate bowl, stir together the reserved plums and the milk, suet, and eggs. Combine with the bread crumb mixture and mix thoroughly.

Grease an 8-cup pudding mold and pour in the batter. Place the pudding (covered tightly) into a steam insert or a double boiler. Steam over medium-low heat for 2 hours.

For the sauce:

Melt the butter in an iron skillet over medium heat. Add the milk and 1 cup of the sugar and simmer until well blended and slightly reduced.

Norman Six shows off some of the produce stored in the Lovitt Restaurant root cellar.

In a small bowl, beat the egg until frothy, then whisk in the remaining sugar and flour until smooth. Slowly add it to the milk-sugar mixture in the skillet, bringing slowly to near boiling point. Stir constantly until the spoon leaves a path on the bottom of the skillet. Remove from the heat, cover, and keep warm on the back of the stove until serving. Unmold the pudding and serve hot with sauce.

Variations: Cooked apples, pears, or cherries can be substituted for the plums.

FALL PANTRY

Crab Apple–Rose Hip Gelée
MAKES ABOUT 3 POUNDS

Crab apples and wild native rose hips are featured on Slow Food's RAFT project for preserving endangered native Northwest flavors. Both are harvested near Quillisascut Farm. The oldest wild-rose fossil in the world was discovered just over the mountain (at Sherman Peak), so our wild roses symbolize the local landscape. Crab apples and roses are related and complement each other well. The gelée can be used on a cheese plate or as a tart filling with walnuts, or can be wrapped in grape leaves with cheese and grilled.

5 pounds crab apples, trimmed of brown spots, stems and blossoms and cut in half

1 pound wild rose hips, trimmed of blossom ends

5 cups organic sugar (evaporated cane juice)

Place the crab apples, rose hips, and sugar in a large pot, cover with water, and simmer until the crab apples are soft—do not drain. Put the mixture through a food mill to remove seeds and skins. Return the mixture to the pot and heat on medium-low. Add 2 cups water, and stir constantly until temperature reaches about 235 degrees F (this takes time, up to an hour). Test occasionally with a candy thermometer.

Pour the mixture onto a baking sheet lined with food-grade plastic wrap and wrap tightly while still warm. When the gelée is cool, it should be sliceable. Gelée can be stored wrapped in an airtight container in the pantry for 2 weeks, or frozen for up to 3 months.

Variations: Quinces or apricots also work well in this recipe. Quince gelée can be used in the Quince and Goat Cheese Cake recipe.

Sauerkraut

MAKES 1 GALLON (16 CUPS)

Store-bought sauerkraut is rarely made by traditional methods, and it just doesn't taste as good as homemade. Traditional sauerkraut requires fermentation, a process that is healthful for human digestion and helps prevent cancer. Most of us don't get enough fermented foods in our diets. Making your own sauerkraut is quite easy, and the result is a buttery, tangy staple that will keep for months. *Note:* For best results, choose a freshly harvested cabbage that is firm and heavy; an older cabbage may not yield the liquid necessary.

  5 pounds cabbage, sliced or grated
  3 tablespoons sea salt

In a large bowl, toss the cabbage with layers of salt. Pack it into a ceramic crock, a food-grade plastic bucket, or a large glass jar, tamping it down hard as you go. Fit a plate or plastic lid snugly inside the crock, and put a clean weight on the cover. This weight should force the water out of the cabbage and keep the cabbage submerged under the brine (the salted water). Cover with a towel.

Periodically press the weight down to force water out of the cabbage. Do this for about 24 hours, or until enough liquid has risen above the cabbage to completely cover it. After 24 hours, if the brine has not risen above the plate level, add enough salt water (1 teaspoon of sea salt dissolved in 1 cup water) to bring the brine level above the plate.

Let the kraut sit in its weighted bucket or jar covered with the towel in a cool, dark place for 2 to 6 weeks. Skim any funk from the brine. Taste the kraut; it will be tangy in the beginning stages and mellow as time goes on. When the flavor is appealing to you, skim the kraut and pack into sterilized glass jars. For optimum health benefits, store in the refrigerator until use. To preserve for long periods, process in a hot water bath for 20 minutes.

Variations: Add shredded carrots, beets, or other root vegetables to the cabbage. Apples, cherries, caraway seeds, or other seeds add color and variation.

Left: Chopped and salted cabbage and carrots are ready to undergo lacto-fermentation to become sauerkraut.
Opposite: Rick harvests cabbage in the fall.

Cured Beef Tongue

MAKES 3–3½ POUNDS

Utilizing uncommon cuts of meat is part of a sustainable kitchen "whole beast" philosophy. Beef tongue is not only economical, it is delicious, nutritious, and simple to prepare. An interesting addition to your charcuterie plate. Lamb tongue may be substituted in this recipe.

1 beef tongue (4 to 5 pounds)

Brine:

    5 quarts (20 cups) water

    1 pound light brown sugar

    3 pounds kosher salt

    1 teaspoon whole black peppercorns

    1 teaspoon dried juniper berries

    6 dried allspice berries (available in the spice
        section of the supermarket)

3 whole cloves

3 dried bay leaves

4 to 5 sprigs fresh thyme

Cooking vegetables:

    1 carrot, peeled, coarsely chopped

    1 yellow onion, peeled, coarsely chopped

    1 leek, coarsely chopped, both white and green part

    5 cloves garlic, smashed

    1 stalk celery, coarsely chopped

    1 teaspoon whole black peppercorns

    5 dried allspice berries

    3 dried bay leaves

    4 to 5 sprigs fresh thyme

For the brine:

In a large saucepan, add the water, sugar, salt, peppercorns, juniper berries, allspice berries, cloves, bay leaves, and thyme. Bring to a boil over medium-high heat, stirring to dissolve the sugar and salt. Boil for 2 minutes, remove from heat, and let steep, covered, for 15 minutes.

Transfer the brine to a stainless steel bowl or glass dish, cover, and refrigerate until cool. When the brine is cool, place the beef tongue in the brine and weight it down with a plate or dish to ensure that the brine covers the tongue completely. Cover and refrigerate for 5 days. Remove the tongue from the brine, rinse well, and reserve for cooking.

For the cooking vegetables:

Place the reserved tongue in a large stockpot and add the carrot, onion, leek, garlic, celery, peppercorn, allspice berries,

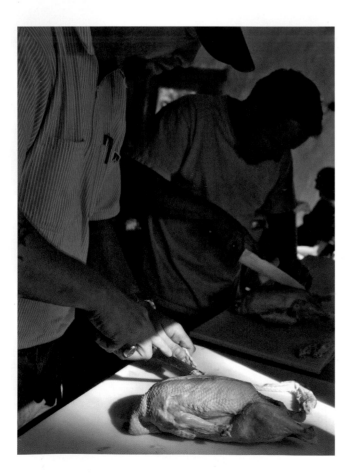

bay leaves, and thyme. Cover with water. Over medium heat, bring to a gentle simmer, cover the pot, and continue to cook for 2½ hours. Test the meat with a skewer—it should pierce easily when done.

Remove the tongue to a cutting board and cool. Discard the cooking vegetables. When the tongue is cool enough to handle, peel the coarse layer of skin off down to the muscle meat; discard extra skin. Serve tongue thinly sliced.

Duck Prosciutto

MAKES ABOUT 3 POUNDS

Air-cured, this is delicious shaved in a salad with arugula, on a baguette with cheese and mustard, or served as part of a charcuterie plate.

6 tablespoons kosher salt

3 tablespoons coarsely ground black pepper

2 tablespoons brown sugar

4 bay leaves, chopped

2 dried arbol chiles, crushed

1 teaspoon cracked cardamom

6 sprigs fresh winter savory, chopped

4 pounds duck breasts, rinsed and patted dry

1 cup brandy or schnapps

In a small bowl, mix together the salt, pepper, brown sugar, bay leaves, arbol chiles, cardamom, and winter savory. Thoroughly coat the duck breasts with this rub. Wrap loosely in parchment paper and place in a shallow pan in the refrigerator for 2 days.

After 2 days, unwrap the duck breasts and gently tap away any loose spices. Tie or hook the breasts to a shelf of the

Farm students Christopher Conville and Tom Loverich fabricate ducks for confit.

refrigerator with a drip pan beneath. Let cure for 1 week.

Rinse the breasts in the brandy and continue to cure in the refrigerator for 2 more weeks. (If your refrigerator is very humid, it may take longer to cure.) When done, the duck will be firm to the touch on the outside and slightly shrunken in appearance. When sliced, it will have an even texture from edge to center. Slice thinly across the grain to serve.

Duck Confit

MAKES 8 SERVINGS

An essential ingredient in our cassoulet, duck confit is easy to prepare and keeps wonderfully for an elegant meal on the fly. Serve it as an entrée, or try flaking it over a bed of braised cabbage. Duck confit is duck that is cured and cooked in its own fat. It must be stored in the fat to keep safely over time. Confit must be gently reheated in the fat to release it from its container. For duck confit flavor to fully develop, confit should be stored for 2 weeks.

For ease in cooking meals for two, consider storing 2 duck hindquarters in 4 Mason jars and pouring fat over before cooling. To serve, heat a Mason jar in a pan of water to melt the fat. Duck fat can be strained and used again, provided it has never reached the smoking point.

    6 to 8 sprigs of fresh thyme
    2 dried bay leaves, chopped
    2 teaspoons freshly grated nutmeg
    1 tablespoon cracked black pepper
    ⅓ cup kosher salt
    8 duck legs, rinsed and patted dry
    3 pounds rendered duck fat

In a small bowl, combine the thyme, bay leaves, nutmeg, pepper, and salt. Rub the duck legs with the mixture and place in a covered glass dish to marinate in the refrigerator overnight.

The next day, preheat the oven to 250 degrees F. Melt the duck fat in a saucepan over medium-low heat. Remove the marinated duck from the refrigerator. Pat the legs dry and pack them tightly in a tall, narrow saucepan or loaf pan. Pour the rendered duck fat over the legs. The duck legs should be completely submerged in fat. Cook, covered, for 3 to 4 hours.

To store, keep the cooked duck legs submerged in fat, place in the refrigerator until ready to use, or freeze in quart jars for up to 3 months. Reheat when ready to use.

To serve, slowly bring the fat up to melting and hot. Remove the duck legs. Sear the duck legs, skin-side down, in a sauté pan over medium-high heat, until crisp. Serve immediately.

Following page: After a long day of working and learning on the farm, it is important to slowly enjoy a meal and good company.

RETHINKING THE KITCHEN

WELCOMING INTO YOUR KITCHEN some of the energy, flavors, good health, and sense of community of Quillisascut Farm doesn't involve physically remodeling your kitchen—just rethinking what you bring into it and how you work with ingredients. What follows is a basic guide to making your kitchen more sustainable through informed purchasing decisions and thoughtful practices in the kitchen.

SEEK ORGANIC, BUY LOCAL

It would be great if we could buy all our foods from local *and* organic sources, but this is not always possible, so we must make informed choices. For instance, Lora Lea likes to buy her grains and flours from farmers such as Fred Fleming, who belongs to Shepherd's Grain, an alliance of several progressive farms in eastern Washington. Even though his farm outside the town of Reardan, near Spokane, is not certified organic, his sustainable and climate-friendly farm practices assure Lora Lea of clean, wholesome food.

Buying from him also gives her a chance to talk directly to the farmer. "It seems like the sustainable-kitchen movement is moving past labels [that is, the U.S. Department of Agriculture (USDA) Organic seal], and that more in-depth knowledge and communication with our farmers is what we need," she says. "Labels can help us when we can't determine for ourselves if a product fits our desires for

a safe healthy future for our children's children." It's true, with the way we eat today it's difficult to know where every piece of produce or meat we buy comes from. When you don't know the source of your food, organic labeling can come in handy; but we shouldn't rely only on the organic label for our information.

THE USDA'S BASIC LABELING GUIDELINES

On October 21, 2002, organic farmers and processors began to use the new USDA Organic seal. Use of the seal is voluntary, but its use, as well as use of the word "organic," on food and other agricultural products requires the producer to meet certain U.S. regulations. Requirements include verification from a certification agency as meeting or exceeding USDA standards. Farmers who gross less than $5,000 from organic products, however, and sell directly to consumers or retailers are exempt from the certification requirement. Those farmers may call their product "organic," but they can't use the new USDA seal.

The USDA Organic regulations prohibit the use of irradiation, sewage sludge, or GMOs (genetically modified organisms) in organic production; reflect National Organic Standards Board (NOSB) recommendations concerning items on the national list of allowed synthetic and prohibited natural substances; prohibit antibiotics in organic meat and poultry; and require 100 percent organic feed for organic livestock. The USDA approved four categories of organic labels; these categories apply to canned and packaged foods as well as to fresh produce, meats, and other food items. Since August 2005, other nonfood items—such as cosmetics and home-cleaning products—can also carry organic labeling based on the percentage of organic content.

Presenting meals in beautiful bowls, platters, and service ware honors the food and the cook.

Some key USDA terminology includes:

100 percent organic. The item meets regulations and may carry the USDA Organic seal.

Organic. At least 95 percent of the content is organic by weight (excluding water and salt); the item may carry the USDA Organic seal.

Made with organic. At least 70 percent of the content is organic, and the front product panel may display the phrase "made with organic," followed by up to three specific ingredients. The item may *not* display the USDA Organic seal.

Less than 70 percent of the content is organic. The ingredi-

ents that are organic may be listed on the ingredients panel only, with no mention of "organic" on the main panel. The item may *not* display the USDA Organic seal.

(*Source:* This information was provided by the Organic Trade Association.)

THE TRUE VALUE OF AN HEIRLOOM

Although the USDA doesn't weigh in on this issue, the Seed Savers Exchange defines an heirloom as "any garden plant that has a history of being passed down within a family, just like pieces of heirloom jewelry·or furniture." But it is not just historical interest that makes heirlooms special. Through the selection of varieties that show resistance to the pests and diseases occurring in the area where they grow, heirlooms increase genetic diversity in the local ecosystem. As important as this is, what most gardeners, and eaters, are interested in is the variety in taste, color, shape, size, and texture of the fruits, vegetables, herbs, and nuts they love to grow and eat.

On the Seed Savers' 890-acre farm in Decorah, Iowa, literally thousands of rare and historical varieties of fruits, vegetables, and herbs are grown in certified organic fields to preserve their seeds for sale to gardeners around the world. In the vegetable gardens more than twenty-four thousand varieties are grown (five hundred types of tomatoes alone are rotated each year!), making this a living museum and laboratory for seed preservation and research. For instance, of the eight thousand varieties of apples that were listed in records as being grown in the United States around 1900, seventy-three hundred have been lost. The organization has obtained seven hundred of the remaining varieties and has planted them in its Historic Orchard, decreasing the chances that they, too, will become extinct.

The term *heirloom* is something of an heirloom itself. It was resurrected and popularized when Kent Whealy,

A burlap bag of heirloom fingerling potatoes is opened in late winter after being stored in the unheated farm school building since the fall harvest.

Dazzling Diversity

This list below represents a small sampling of the number of varieties of heirloom seeds available for each food from Seed Savers Exchange:

Tomatoes, 2,980	Watermelon, 101
Beans, 1,521	Cucumbers, 101
Peppers, 802	Carrots, 72
Peas, 655	Okra, 57
Potatoes, 650	Leeks, 50
Lettuce, 354	Turnips, 49
Squash, 303	Kale, 34
Corn, 265	Beets, 34
Garlic, 240	Swiss chard, 29
Melons, 143	Cabbage, 26
Radishes, 124	Tomatillos, 23
Eggplant, 118	Spinach, 23

cofounder of the Seed Savers Exchange, used it in a speech in 1981 in Tucson, politely asking permission to use the term from another man, John Withee, who had used the term in his Wanigan Associates bean catalog. But Withee said he had borrowed it, too, from University of New Hampshire Professor William Hepler, who in the 1940s had received some beans and used the term to describe them.

THE RISKS OF GENETICALLY MODIFIED SEEDS

Just as heirlooms represent heritage and uniqueness, genetically modified seeds represent newness and monoculture. In 1999 the Council for Responsible Genetics and a coalition of seed companies created the "Safe Seed Pledge," which asks seed companies and other agricultural organizations to commit to not planting genetically modified seeds. The Misterlys, and many other small farmers around the country, have also committed to this pledge, which reads:

"Agriculture and seeds provide the basis upon which our lives depend. We must protect this foundation as a safe and genetically stable source for future generations. For the benefit of all farmers, gardeners, and consumers who want an alternative, *we pledge that we do not knowingly buy or sell genetically engineered seeds or plants.*

"The mechanical transfer of genetic material outside of natural reproductive methods and between genera, families, or kingdoms poses great biological risks as well as economic, political, and cultural threats. We feel that genetically engineered varieties have been insufficiently tested prior to public release. More research and testing is [sic] necessary to further assess the potential risks of genetically engineered seeds. Further, we wish to support agricultural progress that leads to healthier soils, genetically diverse agricultural ecosystems, and ultimately healthy people and communities."

PURCHASING POWER

When stocking your kitchen, consider these terms—*organic, heirloom, non-GMO*—and factor them into your decisions at the grocery store, coop, farmers market, or roadside farmstand. Farmers markets are in full swing at the height of summer, when it is easy to find gorgeous produce and fresh meat. This is also a great time to get to know your farmer, rancher, cheesemaker, or fishmonger. The knowledge you gain from bending an ear when the producer's foods are at their best can help you make more sustainable purchasing decisions year-round, when you visit the local supermarket more often.

Purchasing Meat and Produce

- Contact your local extension agent or local grange, or visit your local farmers market, to find farmers, ranchers, and artisans in your area.
- Consider making your purchases with these criteria in mind: organic *and* local (your first choice), local (your second choice), and organic (your third choice).
- Talk to these farmers, ranchers, cheesemakers, and poultry producers about their farming practices. Ask if they are certified organic or Food Alliance certified. (They may be practicing other standards that are even more stringent than these.) Ask what environmental practices they are using and whether their products are hormone-free.
- Encourage them to sell less common cuts of meat so that entire animals are used and not wasted.
- Research the environmental and health benefits of grass-fed meats.
- Be aware of labeling regulations. Labeling and marketing language on packaging can be deceptive; for example, "natural" has no standardized meaning.
- Keep dollars in your community by shopping at farmers markets and farm stands.
- Purchase produce in quantity at the peak of the season, when it's at its most flavorful and cheapest. Learn such preserving techniques as freezing, drying, pickling, and canning so that you can enjoy the produce year-round.
- Purchase meats in quantity, such as a quarter of a beef, going in with friends or family to share the cost.
- Consider joining a CSA (Community Supported Agriculture) co-op to receive fresh produce delivered to your door, or to pick up at the farmers market or farm. Share with a neighbor to keep from wasting extra food.

Purchasing Seafood

- Regularly look up seafood "watch lists" on the Internet for current information about ocean fisheries issues. Make purchasing decisions that reflect your concerns for endangered fish species or harmful fishing practices. When you dine out, avoid ordering species that are on the watch list, and let the restaurant's manager know you're doing so.

- Be current on farmed fish and shellfish issues. Some aquaculture is considered sustainable, some definitely not. Aquaculture often employs FDA-approved drugs and dyes in fish and shellfish.
- Ask your local purveyor where and when the fish was caught (make him or her show you the "date-caught" tag that comes with each box of fish or shellfish), how it was harvested, and so on. Make sure to follow up when you visit again. This helps to educate your purveyor, who should find out the answers to your questions. It also creates a relationship between you and your purveyor.
- Research the seasonality of fish in your area. When the run is abundant, the costs are lower, and usually the fishery is more viable.
- Learn to cook with flash-frozen (at sea) products so that you can avoid using an aquaculture product during the off-season.
- Learn to preserve seafood by smoking, canning, or pickling, which both extends the season and cuts down on waste.

BUYING SUSTAINABLY FOR THE PANTRY

A cornerstone of sustainability is buying locally grown fresh produce, but in winter that's often difficult. Following are a few tips to help you make more suitable purchasing decisions for your pantry during the dark months.

Fiery hot dried Red Cherry Bomb peppers

- Eliminate from your pantry products made with GMOs. Look particularly at labels of products that contain soy, canola, or corn; if they do not say "organic," they are likely GMO.
- Keep current on GMO products in the marketplace.
- Take it a step further by eliminating all nonorganic products from your pantry.
- How far has each item in your pantry traveled? Check labels to minimize your use of products that have traveled great distances, and instead look for local producers of these products.
- Be creative in finding substitutes for fresh products that must travel long distances. For example, stock your pantry with verjus (the juice from unripened grapes, available bottled at specialty stores, some wineries, and grocers) or sumac (available in Mediterranean markets) to use in place of fresh lemons.
- Purchase in bulk whenever possible to limit the amount of packaging used. Store bulk items properly to prevent waste.
- Keep current on social-justice issues surrounding food, like labor and slavery realities. Look for such key terms as *free trade* or *songbird-friendly* on labels, but be aware that some of these terms are not regulated and can be controversial. Be sure to ask questions of your grocer or other vendor, or research these items yourself on the Internet.
- When buying bottled or canned products, look for those that are locally produced.

WASTE NOT, WANT NOT

While making informed buying decisions puts healthy, flavorful food into our hands and onto the table, incorporating sustainable practices into the work of the kitchen enhances those thoughtful purchases. In the home kitchen, a little reducing, reusing, and recycling can go a long way. Here are a few ways you can make a difference in your community:

- Cut down your use of paper towels by using a salad spinner or washable cloth towels. (Most cotton is genetically modified, so buying organic cotton towels is even better.)
- Consider using reusable coffee and tea filters.
- Purchase composting bins. (Some communities offer them free, so check with your local government.) Compost your coffee grounds, fruit and vegetable peels and trimmings, nutshells, and so on. Use the finished compost in your garden, or donate it to a local community or school garden.
- Find out whether your city recycles cooking oil for use as an alternative fuel.
- Locate a charity or food-retrieval program in your area that will take leftover or unused foods and surplus garden produce.
- Reduce waste by using the whole food product as you cook. For example, if you plan to make a meringue with egg whites, use the yolks later for aioli or custard.
- Plan ahead. Pull frozen goods out of the freezer in ample time for thawing in the refrigerator so that you don't have to run water over them for quick defrosting.
- Keep a log on your refrigerator or freezer to track items that you are storing. List the item, the date you purchased it, and the reason for which you bought it. This system will remind you to use foods before their quality deteriorates and will give you ideas for future meals.

Ultimately, what foods we buy affect the taste and quality of what we make, as well as the health of our home and our community.

Farm fresh peaches will be preserved and provide a bit of summer warmth come January.

MEMBERSHIP ORGANIZATIONS

In recent years many local, national, and international food-focused membership organizations have been created. These organizations hold regular community dinners, educational events, conferences, and workshops and are open to anyone interested in issues of food sustainability, gardening, cooking, and the simple pleasures of the table.

Chefs Collaborative

When we dine out, there is often a huge disconnect between our food and its source. Most restaurant food is supplied by large distributors that ship all over the country. The beef in your hamburger, for example, may have come from a slaughterhouse and packing plant in Ohio; the lettuce may have come from California or Mexico, depending on the time of year. In recent years many chefs have been struggling with how to cook with local, sustainable, and humanely produced foods—and still make a profit. This issue is important to the home cook, too, even though more than half of most Americans' weekly meals are eaten at restaurants.

Chefs Collaborative is a national nonprofit organization of chefs and food lovers alike that supports sustainability in the professional (and the home) kitchen. Chapters in Boston, Portland, and Seattle are active in creating connections between farmers and chefs, holding "meet and greet" events that feature tastings of everything from goat cheese to local shellfish. At one tasting at Pike Brewing Company in Seattle, which featured members of the Pacific Shellfish Growers Association, the public was invited to taste fresh local oysters, clams, and geoduck with organic Pike ales. Charles and Rose Ann Finkel, the owners of Pike Brewing Company, have been supporters of Quillisascut Farm for years, serving their cheeses

The sign says "Farm School," so this must be the place.

in the Pike Pub and organizing tastings. For them, this was a chance to bring together a network of food lovers, chefs, and producers to share their love for local foods.

Chefs Collaborative
262 Beacon Street
Boston, MA 02116
617-236-5200
www.chefscollaborative.org

Slow Food USA

Slow Food is an international nonprofit organization founded in 1986 in Italy by Carlo Petrini, a writer, editor, and activist who was outraged at the opening of a McDonald's on Rome's famed Piazza Spagna. Two decades later, the whole world is talking about "food communities" and the practices of "good, clean, and fair" food. "Sustainable agriculture" has come to be defined as food that is produced in an environmentally sustainable, economically sustainable, and socially just manner. It embodies a value system that was part of the early organic food and farming movement. Now, there are more than 160 Slow Food "convivia," or local chapters, in the United States and 80,000 members around the world.

Since its inception, the Slow Food organization has focused on several publications and on a few major projects. The Ark of Taste is a list of endangered foods, analogous to the list of animals on Noah's Ark. Another project, Presidia, encourages and supports artisan producers. Slow Food is also a major partner in the Renewing America's Food Traditions (RAFT) project (see the "Fall Preservation" chapter). The sustainable food movement has many people examining the true costs of cheap food and learning how to make adjustments in their lifestyle choices. It is a philosophy that puts human beings in context with the web of life and nature's operating system.

But Slow Food isn't just about environmentalism, business, or politics. Its main philosophy is to encourage "the pleasures of the table," bringing people together around local foods and traditions. In the process they learn about how their food systems work and how important it is to protect artisan production and, along with it, taste, history, and culture.

Slow Food USA
434 Broadway, 7th Floor
New York, NY 10013
212-965-5640
www.slowfood.com
www.slowfoodusa.org

Other Sustainable Food Organizations

Lora Lea and the community of Quillisascut Farm are also involved with the following organizations in the Northwest and beyond.

Oregon Tilth
470 Lancaster Drive Northeast
Salem, OR 97301
503-378-0690
www.tilth.org/site/

Rural Roots
P.O. Box 8925
Moscow, ID 83843
206-883-3462
www.ruralroots.org

Seattle Tilth
4649 Sunnyside Avenue North,
Room 1
Seattle, WA 98103
206-633-5045
www.seattletilth.org

Southern Foodways Alliance
Center for the Study of Southern Culture
Barnard Observatory
University, MS 38677
662-915-5993
www.southernfoodways.com

Shepherd's Grain flours used at the farm are grown in
Eastern Washington and Food Alliance approved.

RESOURCES

Dozens of local, regional, and national organizations and websites provide a wide range of information on sustainability, food safety, food labeling, and more. This resource list of books, farm products and seed companies, member organizations, university extension programs, and websites offering seasonal charts and information on food and sustainability represents some of the best sources of reliable, easily accessible information. Use these resources to help you make food choices to support your community and build a healthy and sustainable food system.

Books

Farming with the Wild: Enhancing Biodiversity on Farms and Ranches, by Daniel Imhoff (San Francisco: Sierra Club Books, 2003).

Manifestos on the Future of Food and Seed, by Slow Food Terra Madre (Boston: South End Press, 2007).

Renewing America's Food Traditions, by Renewing America's Food Traditions (RAFT) (Flagstaff, Arizona: Center for Sustainable Environments at Northern Arizona University, 2004)

Renewing Salmon Nation's Food Traditions, by RAFT (Portland, Oregon: RAFT and Ecotrust, 2006).

The Revolution Will Not Be Microwaved: Inside America's Underground Food Movements, by Sandor Ellix Katz (White River Junction, Vermont: Chelsea Green, 2006).

Stella Natura Biodynamic Planting Guide and Calendar, edited by Sherry Wildfeuer (Camphill Village, PA: Kimberton Hills, 2007).

Farm Products and Seed Companies

Bluebird Grain Farms
P.O. Box 1082
Winthrop, WA 98862
509-996-3526
www.bluebirdgrainfarms.com

Cliffside Orchards
P.O. Box 230
Kettle Falls, WA 99141
509 738-6165
www.cliffsideorchard.com

Good Seed Company
195 Bolster Road
Oroville, WA 98844
www.goodseedco.net

Johnny's Selected Seeds
955 Benton Avenue
Winslow, ME 04901
877-JOHNNYS (564-6697)
www.johnnysseeds.com

Lentz Spelt Farms (spelt and emmer grain)
P.O. Box 2
Marlin, WA 98832
509-345-2483
www.lentzspelt.com

McMurray Hatchery
P.O. Box 458
191 Closz Drive
Webster City, IA 50595
515-832-3280; 800-456-3280

Native Seeds/SEARCH
526 North Fourth Avenue
Tucson, Arizona 85705
520-622-5561
www.nativeseeds.org

Nichols Garden Nursery
1190 Old Salem Road Northeast
Albany, OR 97321-4580
800-422-3985
www.nicholsgardennursery.com

Niman Ranch
1600 Harbor Bay Parkway, Suite 250
Alameda, CA 94502
866-269-0642
www.nimanranch.com

Paul's Pastured Poultry
3393 Beck Road
Rice, WA 99167
509-738-3199
www.paulspasturedpoultry.com

Peaceful Valley Farm and Garden Supply
P.O. Box 2209 / 125 Clydesdale Court
Grass Valley, CA 95945
530-272-4769
www.groworganic.com

Puget Sound Fresh
201 South Jackson Street, Suite 600
Seattle, WA 98104
206-296-7824
www.pugetsoundfresh.org

Quillisascut Farm School of the Domestic Arts
Quillisascut Goat Cheese Company
2409 Pleasant Valley Road
Rice, WA 99167
509-738-2011
www.quillisascutcheese.com

Riverview Orchards/Crandall
Coffee Roasters
1521 Highway 25 South
Kettle Falls, WA 99141
509-738-2068
www.crandallcoffee.com

Seed Savers Exchange
3076 North Winn Road
Decorah, IA 52101
563-382-5990
www.seedsavers.org

Shepherd's Grain
Fred Fleming and Karl Kupers
12996 Kupers Road North
Harrington, WA 99134
Fred: 509-979-1162
Karl: 509-721-0374
www.shepherdsgrain.com

Thundering Hooves Pasture-Finished Meats
2021 Isaacs Avenue
Walla Walla, WA 99362
509-522-9400; 866-350-9400
www.thunderinghooves.net

Turtle Tree Seed
Camphill Village
Copake, NY 12516
888-516-7797
www.turtletreeseeds.com

Food Information

American Grassfed Association
877-774-7277
aga@americangrassfed.org
www.americangrassfed.org

American Livestock Breeds Conservancy
P.O. Box 477
Pitttsboro, NC 27312
919-542-5704
www.albc-usa.org

American Pastured Poultry Producers Association
36475 Norton Creek Road
Blodgett, OR 97326
541-453-4557
www.apppa.org

The Bioneers
Old Lamy School House
6 Cerro Circle
Lamy, NM 87540
505-986-0366; 877-246-6337
(1-877-BIONEER)
www.bioneers.org

Cascade Harvest Coalition
4649 Sunnyside Avenue North, Room 123
Seattle, WA 98103
206-632-0606
www.cascadeharvest.org

Center for Sustainable Environments
Northern Arizona University
Gary Paul Nabhan (RAFT Founder and Facilitator)
P.O. Box 5765
Flagstaff, AZ 86011-5765
928-523-0637
home.nau.edu/environment

Community Food Security Coalition
P.O. Box 209
Venice, CA 90294
310-822-5410
www.foodsecurity.org

Council for Responsible Genetics
5 Upland Road, Suite 3
Cambridge, MA 02140
617-868-0870
www.gene-watch.org

Eat Wild
29428 129th Avenue Southwest
Vashon Island, WA 98070
866-453-8489
www.eatwild.com

Melon seedlings are started early in the greenhouse and will be transplanted directly into the ground when warmer temperatures arrive.

Ecotrust
721 Northwest Ninth Avenue, Suite 200
Portland, OR 97209
503-227-6225
www.ecotrust.org

Environmental Defense Fund
257 Park Avenue South
New York, NY 10010
212-505-2100
www.cnvironmentaldefense.org

Farm Aid
P.O. Box 228
Champaign, IL 61824
800-FARM-AID
www.farmaid.org

Food Alliance
1829 Northeast Alberta, Suite 5
Portland, OR 97211
503-493-1066
www.foodalliance.org

Food Lifeline
1702 Northeast 150th Street
Shoreline, WA 98155
206-545-6600
www.foodlifeline.org

GreenerChoices
Consumers Union
101 Truman Avenue
Yonkers, NY 10703-1057
914-378-2000
www.greenerchoices.org

Sivri Biber peppers are stored on the windowsill of the
farm's kitchen, waiting until they are needed in a recipe.

Marine Stewardship Council
2110 North Pacific Street, Suite 102
Seattle, WA 98103
206-691-0188
www.msc.org

The Meatrix Films
www.themeatrix.com
www.moremeatrix.com

Organic Grassfed Beef Coalition
P.O. Box 125
Vermillion, SD 57069
605-638-0748
www.organicgrassfedbeef.org

Pacific Marine Conservation Council (PMCC)
P.O. Box 59
Astoria, OR 97103
503-325-8188; 800-343-5487
www.pmcc.org

Seafood Watch Program
Monterey Bay Aquarium
886 Cannery Row
Monterey, CA 93940
831-648-4800
www.mbayaq.org/cr/seafoodwatch.asp

Sustainable Northwest
813 Southwest Alder, Suite 500
Portland, OR 97205
503-221-6911
www.sustainablenorthwest.org

Tilth Producers of Washington
P.O. Box 85056
Seattle, WA 98145
206-442-7620
www.tilthproducers.org

Washington State Farmers Market Association
P.O. Box 445
Suquamish, WA 98392
206-706-5198
www.wafarmersmarkets.com

Washington Sustainable Food and Farming Network
P.O. Box 762
Mount Vernon, WA 98273
360-336-9694
www.wsffn.org

Whole Grains Council
Oldways
266 Beacon Street
Boston, MA 02116
617-421-5500
www.wholegrainscouncil.org

Wild Farm Alliance
P.O. Box 2570
Watsonville, CA 95077
831-761-8408
www.wildfarmalliance.org

WSDA Farm to Cafeteria
P.O. Box 42560
Olympia, WA 98504
360-902-1884
agr.wa.gov/Marketing/SmallFarm/farmtocafeteria.htm

WWF (formerly the World
Wildlife Fund)
1250 24th Street Northwest
P.O. Box 97180
Washington, D.C. 20090-7180
202-293-4800
www.panda.org

Seasonal Charts
Use these online charts to find out more about what is available in your area during the different growing seasons of the year.

USDA Fruits and Vegetables Analysis
www.fas.usda.gov/htp/fruit_veg.asp

Seasonal Cornucopia (for the Pacific Northwest)
www.seasonalcornucopia.com

Sustainability Information

City Green Building (Seattle)
www.seattle.gov/dpd/GreenBuilding

Cleaning Products
www.worldwatch.org/pubs/goodstuff/cleaningproducts

Ecological Footprint
www.myfootprint.org

The Green Guide
National Geographic Society
www.thegreenguide.com

Green Restaurant Association
www.dinegreen.com/twelvesteps.asp

Recycling, Reuse, and Renewal
www.earth911.org

Goats like to see what's going on around the farm!

World Water Day
www.unesco.org/water/water_celebrations/index.shtml

University Extension Programs

In the Pacific Northwest, several university extension programs provide an amazing amount of printed and online information for cooks, gardeners, farmers, and anyone interested in local foods. Check out university extension programs where you live.

Washington State University (WSU) Extension Programs
Hulbert 411
Pullman, WA 99164-6230
509-335-2837
ext.wsu.edu

Oregon State University (OSU)
Extension Service
108 Ballard Hall
Corvallis, OR 97331-3602
541-737-2713
extension.oregonstate.edu

ACKNOWLEDGMENTS

JUST AS QUILLISASCUT FARM itself is an extended community involving many processes and activities, this book could not exist if it weren't for the generous and able assistance and support of many hands.

My grateful thanks to many friends and colleagues, including the dynamic board (and can-do volunteers) of Chefs Collaborative: Nancy Bardue, Seth Caswell, Meg Chadsey, Michelle Clair, Charles Drabkin, Ashlyn Forshner, Jenn Hall, Nathan Hambley, Craig Hetherington, Kären Jurgensen, Alison Leber, Zachary Lyons, Kristen Schumacher, and others who have grown a small organization into a burgeoning community of chefs, food lovers, farmers, and other artisan producers.

Thank you also to the indomitable dynamic duo of Charles and Rose Ann Finkel, owners of Pike Brewing Company, who generously opened their home to Slow Food Seattle members and helped organize the goat cheese tasting event where I first met Lora Lea and Rick and their goats. Since then, other members of Slow Food have become involved on a national scale, including Gerry Warren, who has spearheaded the inclusion of food items from the Pacific Northwest on the Slow Food Ark of Taste and Presidia. His work is important to all of us.

Thanks to Jon Rowley for his friendship and his unending support of great, fresh food, fish, and wine; to Kate McDermott for her lovely, generous spirit; and to "Oyster" Bill Whitbeck for the steady supply of oysters and mussels needed during the writing of this book.

Pea sprouts are one of the earliest green vegetables in spring. Plant them thick to have plenty of peas later on.

And thank you to the many others who share our love for Quillisascut Farm, including Tom Douglas and his crew of incredible chefs and staff, including Amy Pennington, the producer of Tom's radio show, for her humor and encouragement. Thank you to Erin Fettridge and her crew from Stumbling Goat Bistro, and to the inimitable Christopher Conville, Greg Atkinson, Jennifer McGann, and other chefs whose passion for their work and support of this little farm and other small producers mean everything.

Thanks also to Amy Grondin of the Pacific Marine Conservancy Council and all those working tirelessly to change unsustainable fishing and farming practices. Thanks to Abil Bradshaw, one-woman nutritionist dynamo, and Melissa Flynn, who loves food and appreciates the beauty of Green Lake. Thanks to Christopher Harris for the use of his books and for his pastries; and to Morgan John for his songs and support.

To our editors, Kate Rogers, who first believed in the idea of this book, and Alice Copp Smith, whose attention to detail, sense of humor, and patience with first-timers kept us on track and made this process pleasurable. To Rick and Lora Lea for so generously letting us into their lives, and to Kären Jurgensen and Harley Soltes for their passion and hard work.

I would also like to thank chef, wine lover, and friend Danielle Custer, who has given unceasing support; fellow writer Scott Peterson for his peaceful presence; and my husband and friend, Daniel Randolph, whose love and cheerful support of my work on this book are a gift.

—*Shannon Borg*

We are grateful to all our friends and neighbors for their generous spirits in sharing their stories and the work they are doing to create a prosperous community and healthy planet. Their names are peppered throughout this book—thank you. To the many people not mentioned in this work who have supported the school project from the beginning, we appreciate every one of you.

A few people and organizations need to be specifically thanked: Joanna Moogk; Al Kowitz, director of the Community Agriculture Development Center, Seattle Central Community College Culinary/Baking and Pastry programs; Julia DeVlieg and the DeVlieg Foundation; and Patty Gates and New Priorities Foundation. With your support, we are changing the world!

Most of all, I want to give a standing ovation to all of our students. Without them there wouldn't be a story to tell.

And to Shannon, Kären, and Harley: "Grateful" isn't a big enough word. You have poured all of your life's skill into the production of this book, word by precious word, detail by detail, recipes that took a lifetime of skill and testing to develop, and photos that take my breath away. You have also highlighted for me beauty in so many different ways. Quillisascut Farm is way more than the sum of Rick's and my daily work. This story belongs to all of us; it emphasizes that we are a community. Life is richer having you with whom to share the work. We all share the dream that through this book our readers will find a seed of beauty that they will plant wherever they are—and that we all will have a healthy harvest.

—Lora Lea Misterly

I would like to thank the following people who have inspired, steered, and assisted me in this project: Peter Bonnell, my husband and hero—for his palate, for being my fan, and for his patience and unending accommodation for my "projects"; Aage Bonnell, for being cute and naughty and patient while I tested and typed; Jay Jurgensen, my father and foraging expert, and Lynn and Bill Bonnell. Thanks also to Linda Nee and Chris Jurgensen, for their beautiful garden and inspirational lifestyle, Alice Smith, for her editing skills, support, and humor; Jackie Freeman, Diane Rice, Becky Selengut, and Angela Craft.

Special thanks to the incomparable Christopher Conville because he is.

For their strong arms and big hearts holding Aage while I cooked and processed these recipes, I thank Julie Mullaney, Mitch Rice, Greg Linehan, Alice Aldous, Ashlyn Forschner, Christy Given, Sarah Rice, Marty Bracken, Heidi Linehan, Emily Crawford, Kate Posey, Bernadette Scheller, Marcy Reed, and Jayne Jurgensen.

Thanks to the staff at Seattle Culinary Academy, for their support of Quillisascut Farm and their passion for connecting students with the source of their food and all the issues that come with that; and to FORKS/Seattle Chefs Collaborative board members past and present.

A sincere thank you to all the students, staff, and alumni of the Quillisascut Farm School of the Domestic Arts for their contributions to the farm and this book—in particular, Lynda Oosterhuis, Jennifer McGann, Michelle Clair, Craig Hetherington, Danielle Custer, Melinda Lee, and Rosie Ramirez. Thanks to Don Reed for his constant support of the farm and his passion for bread; and to Karl Vennes, for his generosity to the farm school kitchen and his quest for culinary excellence.

I am grateful to Wilma Jurgensen, my grandmother, for adventures in food, teaching and inspiring me whenever I am in her company; to Daisy Mae Boughey, for her spirit and humor and for housing me in the summertime; to Harley and Shannon who gave this experience visuals and voice. And finally, to Rick and Lora Lea for inviting me into their lives—dull knives, foibles, insecurities, loves, life changes, and all—for helping me to grow, learn, and thrive in their company and with the farm school project.

—Kären Jurgensen

Following page: Chef Kären and a student remove loaves from the wood-fired oven during an evening baking session.

INDEX

A published poet who holds an MFA in poetry from the University of Washington, as well as a PhD in poetry and literature from the University of Houston, **Shannon Borg** regularly writes about travel, food, and wine in the Pacific Northwest. She is certified by the International Sommelier Guild and is a former board member of Slow Food Seattle and Chefs Collaborative's Seattle chapter, and is committed to promoting sustainable cuisine.

Lora Lea Misterly and her husband Rick bought land near Rice, Washington, in 1981 and began selling their cheese in 1987. They now produce roughly 5,000 pounds of farmstead cheese per year, made with the milk from their herd of 35 dairy goats. In 2002 they founded the Quillisascut Farm School of the Domestic Arts, with a focus on teaching culinary students and professionals about the farm-to-table connection. Today, more than 80 student and professional chefs visit their farm each summer.

Lora Lea is deeply dedicated to Tilth Producers, Rural Roots, Washington Sustainable Food and Farming Network, Chefs Collaborative, and Seed Savers Exchange. She is also a founding member and leader of Slow Food Upper Columbia, as well as a team member for the Northwest RAFT project.

Chef Kären Jurgensen grew up in rural Republic, Washington, where her grandmother took her on her first foraging adventures. In addition to her work at the Farm School, Kären is a chef instructor at Seattle Culinary Academy, a mercenary cook, and a restaurant consultant in Seattle. She founded the Seattle chapter of Chefs Collaborative (aka FORKS) and is actively involved in local food politics, the regional Food Policy Council, Women Chefs and Restaurateurs, Les Dames d' Escoffier, and Slow Food's RAFT project.

Award-winning photographer **Harley Soltes** was on staff at the *Seattle Times* for twenty-two years, working on an array of international, domestic, and regional photo assignments including hundreds of cover stories for its Sunday magazine. A freelancer since 2005, he has photographed stories for *LIFE, Sports Illustrated, TIME, People,* and the National Geographic Society. He continues his work as a photojournalist while running a farm in Kingston, Washington.